A RECIPE FOR JOY

The elements of happiness are simple and accessible. In THIS WAY TO HAPPINESS, CLYDE M. NARRAMORE examines the resources that are available to us and explains how you can dramatically change your life to one of contentment and pride.

HOW TO LEARN LOVE
HOW TO ACHIEVE SUCCESS
HOW TO HANDLE FEAR
KNOWLEDGE AND SATISFACTION
THE SECRET OF BELONGING

are among the absorbing and inspiring principles of joy explored in this highly readable, acclaimed, and satisfying bestseller.

OTHER BOOKS BY DR. NARRAMORE . . .

The "Christian Psychology" Series

How to Tell Your Children About Sex

How to Understand and Influence Children

Life and Love

The Psychology of Counseling

This Way to Happiness

A Woman's World

Young Only Once

Encyclopedia of Psychological Problems

Counseling Youth

THIS WAY TO HAPPINESS

Psychology for Living

Clyde M. Narramore, Ed.D.

OF THE ZONDERVAN CORPORATION | GRAND RAPIDS, MICHIGAN 49506

THIS WAY TO HAPPINESS

A ZONDERVAN BOOK
Published by Pyramid Publications for
Zondervan Publishing House

Zondervan Books edition published March 1969
Twenty-ninth printing 1978
ISBN 0-310-29942-X

Printed in the United States of America

ZONDERVAN BOOKS are published by
Zondervan Publishing House, 1415 Lake Drive, S.E.,
Grand Rapids, Michigan 49506, U.S.A.

ACKNOWLEDGMENTS

THIS WAY TO HAPPINESS has grown out of a desire of many people to consider the relationship of vital Christianity to psychology. I am indebted to many individuals and groups throughout America who have encouraged me to write and speak on this subject. Without their inspiration I am sure this book would never have been written.

Grateful appreciation is extended to Dr. Harvey C. Roys for his quotations from *God and the Emotions.* Dr. Gilbert L. Little and Moody Press have graciously given permission to use materials from Dr. Little's publication, *Nervous Christians.* Appreciation is also expressed to Dr. Richard Halverson for thoughts from his weekly publication, *Perspective.*

A special thanks is given to Sylvia Locke and Marion Ferguson for their splendid work on the manuscript, and to Mr. and Mrs. Edwin A. Elliott for their contribution in editing all material.

Loving appreciation is extended to my wife for her months of planning, research, writing and editing in connection with this project.

SIGNS ALONG THE WAY

1
The Search for Happiness

EVERYONE wants to be happy. And people the world over are devising ingenious methods and going in every direction to find happiness. In fact, much of our amazing space age progress is the result of man's search for a happier life.

Men of the twentieth century hold several distinctions. One is their unusual understanding of the human mind and body. This knowledge outstrips that of all other generations. But strangely enough, the more they know about themselves, the less happy they seem to be.

Surely, something is lacking. Because the "things" that many people seek to bring them happiness do not seem to "do the job." With our modern means of earth and space travel, man has still not found his way to happiness. Millions of hospital beds are added each year, but people feel no better. Although an impressive array of clever labor-saving devices give him more leisure time, still he is not content. Today we have more and better foods on the market, yet people are starving for satisfaction. Insurance companies are issuing more policies with wider coverage, but people feel more insecure than ever. Millions are adding tranquilizers to their regular diets, yet they have no peace.

Why is this?

Obviously people are overlooking something important—the ingredients of happiness!

When skilled psychologists and psychiatrists probe into the innermost feelings of man, they find basic psychological needs that demand fulfillment. Just as people have physical necessities—food, shelter and clothing, so they have definite psychological needs. "People," the specialists agree, "cannot possibly function at their best, or find *real happiness until these needs are met.*"

What are these needs? And how are they satisfied?

As you identify your psychological needs and take steps to meet them, you will say, "THIS IS THE WAY TO HAPPINESS."

2

Love and Affection

LITTLE JOHNNIE leaned into the whipping wind as he walked cautiously on the ice coated sidewalk. It was slippery. And it was cold—a biting, stinging cold. Johnnie gripped his jacket tightly around his neck and slid his tousled head low into the upturned collar. Every breath froze before him in the cold morning air. This was winter in Chicago, and Johnnie was on his way to Sunday school. Since carfare money was scarce, he walked the three miles. But rain or shine, hot or cold, Sunday after Sunday, Johnnie was always in his place at Sunday school.

This morning it was colder than usual. But the weather didn't stop Johnnie. He tramped on, block after block, passing by many churches and Sunday schools. Some were large, others small, but Johnnie kept on going.

As he rounded the corner of a large building, he dodged into the entry way to escape the wind and catch his breath for a moment. But someone else had beat him to it. For as he swung around the corner, he almost bumped into a tall man standing against the wall. The man held his hat on his head with one hand and a Bible in the other.

He smiled at Johnnie and said, "Hello, son. Where are you going on this cold morning?"

"To Sunday school," the boy replied.

"Fine," the man said, "I teach a Sunday school class myself. May I ask *where* you attend?"

"Oh, I go to Mr. Moody's Sunday school."

The man looked surprised. "That's a *long* way from here," he said. "Why don't you come to *my* Sunday school this morning. It's much closer and you won't have to walk so far. It's awfully cold, you know."

"No thanks, mister," Johnnie answered.

"Why not?" the teacher persisted.

"I'd rather not," the boy replied. "I wanna go to Mr. Moody's Sunday school."

When the teacher saw that he could not persuade the boy to go elsewhere, he asked him why he went so far through the cold just to be in Mr. Moody's Sunday school.

Johnnie looked up at the man with all his boyish sincerity. "Well, mister," he said, "it's 'cause they *love* a fella over there!"

And Johnnie's reason was a good one. People are willing to go to the ends of the earth to find *love*. To be loved and wanted is a basic psychological need that surges in the heart of every human being. It is the "sweet mystery of life"—and *all* the world is seeking it.

There is an old saying, "Love makes the world go 'round."

In a sense, this is true. It not only makes it go around—but it makes it go around *right*. One can never be his best if he is not loved and wanted. From the time he is a tiny baby in his mother's arms until he becomes an elderly man, one needs to feel that he is valued and loved. Love adds zest to living, and it keeps one at his best so that he does not yield to undue stress and strain.

Those who have given and accepted love and affection find it easy to love others. They are confident, relaxed and happy. They are more likely to have faith in people and get along well with them. In short, love draws the best out of a person. It is the foundation of a good personality. It makes a person joyful and optimistic, And when one feels that he is loved, he sees the world as a challenge—not as a threat. Yes, love is a basic ingredient in happy living. Little wonder then that people search for it the world over.

Yet there are many lonely and unloved people. Mrs. Landis, a teacher, was one of them. As a psychologist, I was asked on several occasions to visit her class for the mentally retarded. She was an outstanding teacher and I often complimented her for the fine work she did. I noticed, too, how much she appreciated it.

At the close of the school year Mrs. Landis came to my office.

"I want to thank you," she said, "for the encouragement you have given me this year." Then with tears filling her eyes she continued, "You may not believe it, Dr. Narramore, but as a child no one ever showed me much kindness. There was no one to love me. And I was grown before anyone ever told me that he or she cared for me. In fact, I often wondered whether I was worthy of notice or attention, and it has bothered me all my life. That's why your encouragement has meant so much to me."

And Mrs. Landis is only one of many. In fact, the key that unlocks most hearts is the one marked, "Love and affection."

When Love Is Not There

Have you ever unravelled an old, worn-out baseball to see how it was made? You pull the string, unravelling it until it is only half size, then you unravel some more until you come to the little rubber ball in the very center. There you can clearly see that the kind of ball you have depends upon what goes into it and how it is constructed.

When psychologists analyze people they do something similar. Through various tests, individual histories and discussions, they can follow the development of a person from early chldhood. They discover what has gone into a person to make him the way he is; they uncover the circumstances that have contributed to his personality. And as they unravel a person's past experiences, they take a careful look at the love and affection that has gone into his life. Have people shown him love and affection? Was it consistent? Who loved him? Was the love genuine and spontaneous? Did they love him for himself or was it for what he could do? How did people express their love to him?

The reason psychologists delve into such an analysis is to help them understand the "why" of behavior. It reveals the motives behind the actions. It is a way of learning the reasons people act the way they do.

And since love is so important, it cannot be overlooked. If the need for love is *not* met in a person's life, he may develop attitudes and tendencies which will affect his entire personality. And he may resort to behavior that will shape his whole life in a distorted pattern.

Consider, for example, people who are always *suspicious* of others. Many times it is because their lives have been robbed of love and affection. If they had known genuine, wholesome love, they would have little cause to be suspicious. But since they have tasted little or no love themselves, they distrust others. Naturally, they tend to look at the future through the same glasses with which they have seen the past. This makes it difficult to accept cordiality and friendliness on its own merit. So even when others do show an interest in them, they suspect that it is fostered by ulterior, selfish motives. This is an uncomfortable, unpleasant feeling. But there are many people who live with it every day. For example, a lady told me not long ago that whenever she saw two or more people talking, she always wondered if they were talking about her. This woman had been raised on a meager diet of love. And because of this undernourished facet of her life, she always imagined the worst. Why? Because her past experiences kept telling her, "They don't care for you."

Then there is *jealousy*. This does not just happen. There are reasons why people are jealous. Often a reason is lack of affection. A person who senses this lack often compares himself with others. Others have received love—but he was deprived of it. Since he wanted to be loved more than anything else in the world, he resents the fact that others were given what he was denied. And he becomes jealous. And what would happen to a group of children if some were given food while others stood by hungry? It would be inevitable: jealousy. Yet the same thing is taking place every day. Many are starved, not from lack of food—but from lack of love. Is it surprising then, that jealousy creeps in? Naturally, it is only a matter of time before these unloved people transfer their feelings of jealousy from one person to another.

Some people find it *difficult to love anyone*—even those dearest to them. This may stem from the fact that they have never been loved themselves. On the other hand, those who have been raised in an environment of warmth and affection find it easy to express their love to others.

Love is learned. The ability to give and recieve affection is something that is acquired. It grows and develops as a person lives with those who express their love to each other. A child who is raised in a family where there is a warm, cordial relationship soon learns to be a warm, cordial person. But when a youngster is brought up in a home where love is scarce, he looks upon affection as a strange, peculiar thing—something that makes him feel uncomfortable and ill at ease.

Not long ago a husband talked to me about this very thing. He could not see the necessity of expressing his love to his wife.

"She's always complaining," he said, "that I don't love her."

"But you *do*," I commented.

"Of course I do," he assured me, "but she seems to think that if I don't go into ecstacies about it, I don't love her.

"I don't know," the husband continued, "but maybe it's because she was raised in a family where they were all very close. In fact, even now when they see each other they still kiss and make a lot over each other. But my family was different. We never acted that way. Oh, we liked each other okay, but we didn't say anything about it. I don't ever remember my Dad hugging or kissing me. And Mom—well, she was a good woman and I know she loved us but she never said much about it. I guess that's the reason I don't make a fuss over my wife. I like her, but that's that. I don't go for this 'gushing' business."

There are many people like this husband. They don't show affection because it is something they have never *learned* to do. And to them it feels strange and unnecessary.

How unfortunate when people have never learned to love! Not only do they make poor marriage partners, inadequate parents and meager members of society—but they miss so much themselves.

Those who have never received much love and affection sometimes react in rather strange ways. Some people spend much of their time trying to *assure themselves that they are worthy of love*. They go to all extremes—make unusual overtures to get others to like them—perhaps even come right out and ask if people love them. Very often they turn the conversation so that the ones with whom they are talking can compliment them. If their friends don't take the hint, they compliment themselves. And then they ask their friends to join in the compliment.

A man once asked me about an acquaintance of his.

"I don't understand her at all," he said. "She's always bragging on herself—tells everyone how good she is. I always figured it was a superiority complex. But now I'm beginning to wonder. Maybe it's the opposite. Maybe she's starved for love and attention so she tries to get it this way. But I do know this, she's smart enough to know better."

I imagine the fellow had it "figured out" about right. When a person has missed out on love and affection he keeps trying to convince himself that he is worthy of it. When this happens, the I.Q. seems to take a back seat. His need may be so strong that he by-passes an intelligent approach.

I have known some prominent men and women whose lives have been void of any real love and affection. Even though they may have had recognition and respect, they have not had love. And it is not uncommon for these people to act in somewhat peculiar ways in an attempt to win the love and affection that they crave so deeply.

Life is a series of *decisions*. From the time we begin reaching for certain toys, we show our preferences. And since choices result in courses of action, our happiness depends upon them.

Have you ever wondered why some people make such poor choices? Oh, they may be intelligent enough. But they don't make intelligent decisions. There are a number of reasons for this. One may be the fact they are grasping for love and affection. Seem strange? It is strange. Nevertheless, it is often true.

When a person has never received much love, the void may be so strong that it colors all his thinking, even when he is making important decisions. He may weigh the facts, then completely disregard them in favor of something that promises some recognition and affection. His emotions are stronger than his reason.

Like a group of young children choosing sides for a ball game. If the chooser is a youngster who is starved for love, he is likely to by-pass the good ball players and choose someone whom he thinks will be a good friend to him. It short, his strong need for affection keeps him from choosing team members who can win the game. His decision is dictated by his inner needs.

And this trait carries over into adulthood. Grownups also let their maladjustments make poor decisions for them. Take Bill White, for example. He is a father, but he refuses to discipline his own children. Why? The basic reason is rather subtly hidden. But it is this: Bill has never been genuinely loved. And he feels that if he disciplines his children, he will lose their affection. And Bill can't afford to run such a risk. He feels that he must hold on to this one thread of love—at all costs.

I have seen similar examples in the classroom—teachers who could not maintain good classroom discipline simply because they were trying to "hold on" to the friendship of their students. These teachers' only love relationship was with their students—and they dared not sever it.

I'm sure you have seen certain couples, and wondered, "How did those two ever get together? Little in common, so completely different. And one has so much more ability than the other."

The answer often lies in the fact that one, or both, suffered from lack of love. This drive over-shadowed all other considerations. Anyone who offered some temporary love and affection was willingly accepted, even though it was a very poor match.

So it is that some people make unwise decisions. Their minds are controlled by a lack in their hearts.

When affection is withheld from people it sometimes shows up in the form of *aggressive behavior*. Since they have not been loved they feel that they have missed out on something which all human beings deserve. They resent this "discrimination." "Others are loved," they reason, "but I've been left out. I'll show them."

So they retaliate.

Feeling that they have a right to "get even" with

society, they devise many ways of "punishing" and "striking out" against people.

I was reminded of this one Monday morning when the head secretary of our staff of psychologists stepped into my office and introduced Miss Peters, the new filing clerk. As they left the room and were passing the filing cabinets in the hallway, I heard Miss Peters ask, "Which cases are filed here?"

"These," the secretary explained, "are all behavior problems—boys and girls who have not been able to adjust to the regular classroom."

"My," exclaimed the new clerk, "there are certainly a lot of them."

"Yes," said the secretary, "but these are just a few; we have them filed under twelve classifications, and these represent only one group."

Miss Peters sighed. "You never think about so many people being in trouble until you work in a place like this."

How true, I thought. And it would be serious enough if this were the only office where thousands of cases of unhappy people were filed. But actually it is only one of many in *every section of the nation.* Children's problems, marriage problems, court cases—an unending list. And at the heart of most of them smoulders a common cause, lack of love and affection.

Not everyone "strikes out" against society for depriving them of love and affection. Some react by *withdrawing.* They feel that they are probably not worthy of love—since they have never received it. So they belittle themselves and pull into their shells.

It is difficult for a person to build *self-confidence* and poise if he feels that he does not merit love. Love and affection are a dynamic impetus in spurring people on to greater self assurance.

Not long ago I counseled with a lady who was suffering from times of mental depression. After several sessions, it became apparent that among other things this lady had been robbed of her self-confidence. I found that her parents had left her when she was only a small child. This was bad enough, but then she was "boarded out" to another family who didn't genuinely care for her. From there she was shuttled from one foster home to another. No one spent time building up her confidence. Rather, they tore it down. No one really loved her.

Finally she withdrew into a make-believe world—one that was much more pleasant than the real world. Here she attempted to avoid the grim reality of being forsaken and unloved.

There are many people like this. Their lack of self-confidence can be traced to lack of love and affection. And whether it is merely an annoying factor or whether it leads to a serious maladjustment, the price of being unloved is too high.

People who have never experienced much love and affection may show this lack in a variety of ways. But after studying many cases, I am convinced of this: regardless of their behavior, they always accept *some* kind of substitute for love. Love is something humans cannot do without. So when it is not within their reach, they turn to something else—even though it is a counterfeit. It may be harmful, but they take it anyway because the basic need for love and affection keeps crying out for some kind of satisfaction.

"Bob" was an example of a fellow living on substitutes. I can still see him as he walked into my office. About twenty-one, he was tall, masculine and alert. His eyes shifted around the room, then settled on me.

Suspecting Bob of using and peddling dope, the police had planted a "girl friend" at a local drive-in. She played the game just right. On their second "date" in his car, he handed her the reefer she had been begging for. She "bumped" the horn, and suddenly, from out of nowhere two officers flashed their lights on the couple, arrested Bob and locked him up in the county jail.

After a preliminary hearing the courts ordered his family to find psychological help for him. So here he was in my office.

After a few sessions Bob began to see how his trouble started. He was starved for love and affection and felt that no one had a place for him. So he joined a gang. As time went on, he got a little of what he had always wanted—friendship and affection. But this "love-substitute" carried a terrible price tag—minor crimes, needles, arrest, shame and a possible prison term, plus a host of other vile things. But he was willing to take the chance just to have the recognition and love that his heart so badly craved.

Many cases are not as severe as this dope addict. But some are. It is not unusual for young men and women to sell their souls and bodies for some attention, even though the love and attention will only last for a few weeks or even a few hours.

People seeking love and affection get into organizations and groups that are very harmful to them, but they are willing to take a chance because they feel they will be loved and appreciated. In their desire for love and affection they search in every direction. If they can't get the real thing, *any substitute* will do.

Many people do not go to such precarious extremes. But they still feel the need to compensate for a lack of love in their lives. So they adopt other mild substitutes as their love objects. It may be a pet that bridges the gap. All their love and affection is showered upon a mere animal. Pets can be a real pleasure. But when people go "overboard" about them, the situation becomes unwholesome and unnatural. Animals are wonderful and they can be our friends—but they should never take the place of human beings.

When love is not there! The symptoms are many. They may include suspicion, jealousy, inability to love others, unwise decisions, aggressive behavior, lack of self-confidence and love substitutes. These and many more—when love is not there.

OTHERS

The story is told about a young lady who fancied herself to be a poetess. In an effort to have her poems accepted for publication, she made the rounds of the various publishing companies. Although she trekked from one editorial offce to another, she seldom got past the secretaries. At last she was granted an interview with the editor of a large, national magazine. Her heart pounded nervously as the receptionist ushered her into his office. She was confident in the excellence of her poetry but she knew that her big task was to "sell" the editor.

As soon as she was seated by his desk, the editor asked specifically what she had in mind. She told him that she had composed some poetry she would like to have published in his magazine.

"Poetry? About what?" asked the editor.

"All about *love,*" she replied.

"Hmmm," mumbled the editor. Then pointedly he asked, "Well, *what is love*? Tell me."

Now was the time to sell. The girl lifted her eyes in a rapturous gaze. "Love," she sighed, "Is filling one's soul with the beauties of the night, by the shimmering moonbeams on the lily pond when the fragrant lilies are in full bloom, and—"

"Stop, stop, stop!" cried the editor curtly. "You are all wrong—very, very wrong. I'll tell you what love is: It's getting up cheerfully out of a warm bed in the middle of the night to fill hot water bottles for sick children. That's real love. I'm sorry, but I don't think we can use your poems."

The editor was right. Love is more than fanciful dreams. When translated into everyday living, love means unselfishness, it means kind and thoughtful deeds. Love is a manner of life.

When I was a boy my mother used to say, "Talk is cheap." And she wasn't far wrong. It is much easier to *say* we love other people than it is to *show* it by the kind things we do. But if we are to help other people meet this basic psychological need—the need for love and affection—we must *do* something about it.

Missionaries from Africa brought back the story of a little native girl who had been sold as a slave. She had never known what love was. Even her name, Keodi, meant "Nobody loves me!"

Keodi's life was hard and bitter. Then when she was nearly ten years old, she contracted a skin disease which covered her body with repulsive sores. The natives turned her out of the village. They would have nothing to do with the poor, sick child.

Then the missionaries took the rejected girl in, bathed her, fed her, cared for her sores, and clothed her. At first she could not believe that anyone really loved her.

"Nobody loves me," she would say. "I am only Keodi."

The missionaries patiently explained over and over again that Jesus loved her. And they tried to *show* her that they loved her.

Then one day she looked down at her dress, her clean body, her bandaged sores. "Is this love?" she asked.

And Keodi had learned the meaning of love. Love is shown by kindness, by doing, and by giving. And as the song writer states it, "What we *do* speaks so loud that the world can't hear what we say!"

There is no better way to show others that we love them than to *give* of ourselves. Giving of *things*, as fine as that may be, is never a substitute for giving our time, our attention, our interest, our affection—*our-*

selves. And true giving has no strings attached: we give because we love.

What are the attributes of love? How can we show others that we love them? By following the simple, yet thorough guide in God's Word. "Love is very patient, very kind. Love knows no jealousy; love makes no parade, gives itself no airs, is never rude, never selfish, never irritated, never resentful; love is never glad when others go wrong, love is gladdened by goodness, always slow to expose, always eager to believe the best, always hopeful, always patient" (I Cor. 13:4-8—Moffatt's translation). This is the ideal set before us: it is *living* our love for others.

But to love without saying so is not enough. People need to be *told* they are loved. Children and adults alike want to be constantly reassured that they are loved and appreciated. A wife may ask her husband, "Honey, do you love me?" She may know full well that he does, but it is reassuring to hear him say it again—and again.

It is unkind and thoughtless to leave our loved ones in doubt as to our affection for them. And it is unnecessary. Only recently I worked with a teenage boy who was having serious problems. As we talked I raised the question as to whether his parents loved him. He looked up and said, "I don't know, but if they do, they've never told me." How sad. They may have loved him—and perhaps they thought he should know. But it never pays to take love for granted.

Many people make this mistake. They excuse themselves from any display of affection by saying, "I'm good to him (or her). He *knows* I love him. Why say more?" So they never put their feelings into words. Naturally, the one on the receiving end wonders, "Does he love me, or not?"

Not long ago a letter came to my desk from a husband whose heart was crying for some love and affection. "I think my wife really loves me," the husband wrote, "but it's hard to tell. She seems to think that since she keeps the house clean, cooks good meals and sews on buttons—that is enough."

That isn't enough. There are many things more important in life than keeping house and cooking meals—there are things much more vital than earning a living and driving a fine car. King Solomon wisely said, "Better is a dinner of herbs where *love is*, than a stalled ox and hatred therewith." (Prov. 15:17).

True, actions *do* speak louder than words. And if there needed to be a choice, deeds would be the more virtuous of the two.

But a choice is *not* necessary. Showing a person that you love him and telling him so, are very compatible partners. Yes, love needs to be expressed in language—as well as in behavior.

If you have a friend worth loving,
Love him. Yes, and let him know
That you love him, ere life's evening
Tinge his brow with sunset glow.
Why should good words ne'er be said.
Of a friend—till he is dead? *Anonymous*

So if you love your "neighbor"—as yourself—you'll not only show him that you love him by the things you do, but you'll tell him too.

The Greatest Love

The story is told of a strange, yet true incident that occurred in Scotland some years ago. A quaint little Highland village lay nestled between the barren cliffs of the rugged Scottish mountains. Many of the villagers earned their living by working in the fields while the small children played nearby and the babies slept in baskets.

One morning a gigantic eagle swooped down upon the field and snatched away a sleeping infant. The whole village pursued it, but the eagle soon perched itself upon a lofty mountain crag and everyone despaired of the child's life.

A brave sailor tried to climb the ascent, but it was too steep and too dangerous and he was forced to give up. A robust Highlander who was a veteran climber also tried to scale the mountain, but neither could he make it.

At last a poor peasant woman tried to climb the dangerous ledge. Risking her life, she clutched the sheer rocks and bravely edged her way higher and higher until she finally climbed to the very top of the cliff. Then, while the tense onlookers below waited with abated breath, she slowly made her way down step by step until at last, amid the shouts and cheers of the villagers, she reached the bottom of the mountain, holding the baby in her arms.

Why did the woman succeed when the strong seaman and the experienced Highlander failed? Why? Because of *love*. That woman loved the baby with a strong love —she was his mother.

Yes, a mother's love is strong. A mother loves her children when the whole world turns against them. Many poems and songs have been written about the love of a mother. The world believes that mother-love is the greatest of all.

But there is a love that is greater. Yes, greater than *all* others. A love that caused the sinless Son of God to climb the hill of Calvary that He might die for our sins. Human love is nothing when compared to the greatness of God's love. It is beyond our limited comprehension. But this we know: when God loves, He loves a *world* —when He gives, He gives His *Son*. "For God so loved the world that He gave His only begotten son that whosoever believeth on Him shall not perish but have everlasting life" (John 3:16). Such is the boundless love of the eternal Father.

You can depend on the love of God. Nothing can deprive you of it. No evil, no transgression—nothing you can do (except to refuse His Son) is bad enough to shut you off from the love of God. You cannot escape His love. It reaches to the farthest corner of the universe —into every nook and cranny, every crack and crevice.

God's love is constantly, continually, eternally dependable for it is based upon God's character. God loves . . . because HE IS LOVE! (I John 4:8).

Human love is different. Man loves the lovely—has almost no capacity to love the unlovable. Man's love depends on the one being loved. God's love depends on the character of Himself. For God not to love is to be untrue to His own nature. If there were to be one man anywhere, any time in history whom God did not love for any reason whatsoever would mean that God is inconsistent. If it were possible for any man to commit a deed so terrible that God could not love him, God would not be *love*.

God's love is not conditional. He does not love us because we are lovable. He does not love us because we are good.

When Dr. Harry Ironside was a small boy he attended a missionary rally where he learned this great truth. The speaker, a missionary from Africa, turned to where Ironside sat with a group of boys and said, "Now boys, I want to tell you the kind of Gospel we preach to the people in Africa. How many good boys have we here?"

"A lot of us thought we were good," Dr. Ironside said, "but since our mothers were there, not one of us dared hold up our hands."

"Well," said the missionary, "not one good boy here; then I have the same message for you that we have for the heathen in Africa; God loves *naughty* boys."

Mr. Ironside thought, *he is all mixed up*, for you see he had heard people say, "If you are *good*, God will love you." Then as the speaker continued, Dr. Ironside found out that those people were wrong. God does not love us only when we are good. And He is not waiting for us to be good so that He can love us; *God loves sinners*. "God commendeth his love toward us, in that, while we were yet sinners, Christ died for us" (Rom. 5:8).

Yes, God's love is constant and consistent. And it is available—now and for eternity. Yet you may miss it simply because you ignore it. And worse yet, refuse it. There is only one thing that a man can do to deprive himself of God's love: He can *reject* it. For love cannot coerce, it cannot force, otherwise it would not be love. Love woos—and waits. And it is up to the beloved to receive it.

God's love is persistent, passionately pure, impartial, inexhaustible and everlasting. It is for every man. It is for YOU—for me. But it is up to us to accept His gift of love, His Son, Jesus Christ. When we do, we are safe in His love—*forever*.

Do you have difficulty believing that God loves you so greatly? Then it is probably because you have never experienced His love. Those who have tasted nothing greater than human love can not understand the love of God.

This was true of Tom. We were shipmates in the U.S. Navy. He was a clean-cut fellow, in his twenties, highly intelligent, married, and the father of a four-year-old girl.

One night as we were standing watch together, chatting about one thing or another, the conversation turned to God.

"I don't understand what God is all about," he said.

"What do you mean?" I asked.

"Well," he said, "I don't see how God could pay attention to individual people. And even if He did, I don't see how He could *love* them."

"Tom," I said, "God is *not* like we are. His nature is such that He knows *each* of us, and He is interested in us *individually*."

"But how can He *love* us?" Tom inquired.

"Well, Tom," I explained, "there is really nothing with which we can compare God's love. About the best love we know is that of a parent for his child. For example, you've told me about your little girl, Joy."

Tom's eyes lighted up. If there was anyone who was especially dear to his heart, it was his little Joy. Several times he had shown me her picture and I knew he loved her dearly.

"Tom, you love Joy, don't you?"

"Oh," he said, "I love her more than I can tell you." Then with a look of real sincerity, Tom said, "I'd gladly die for that little tyke."

"All right," I continued. "You love her so much that you would do *anything* for her. Now let me ask you something: Where does all love come from? Who invented love? Who is the source of all love?"

"I don't know," Tom said, "I've never thought about that."

"All love comes from God," I explained. "He is the One who created love. God *is* love. And He is the One who makes it possible for us, His creatures, to love.

"Tom," I continued, "the love you have in your heart for your wife and your little girl is nothing compared to God's love for you! Human love is only a thimble full. But God's love is like a great, inexhaustible ocean. He can love us a million times more than we can love each other. He is the *source* of all love!"

Tom sat quietly for a minute, mulling it over in his mind. Then he spoke, "Now I see it . . . But how do we *know* He loves us so much?"

"God's love is manifested to us in a thousand ways," I said, "But the only *real* way to know, is to *experience* it."

"How do you do that?" he asked.

"Just let Him love you." Then I turned to some verses in the Bible that showed us how much God loves us: "In this was manifested the love of God toward us, because that God sent His only begotten Son into the world, that we might live through Him" (I John 4:9). "Herein is love, not that we loved God, but that He loved us and sent His Son to be the propitiation [mercy seat] for our sins" (I John 4:10). "Hereby perceive we the love of God, because He laid down His life for us' (I John 3:16).

God was speaking to Tom. And he was beginning to understand.

"Now, Tom," I continued, "through the Bible you can *learn* that God loves you. But through accepting Christ as your personal Saviour, you can *experience* His love. Some years ago I did this very thing. I saw that God loved me. Then I asked Christ to come into my heart and save me. I asked Him to forgive my sins, and I placed my trust in Him. Immediately, like a miracle, He quietly took up His abode in my heart. And through the years God's love has become more and more real to me.

"Wouldn't you like to experience His love?" I asked.

With tender heart he looked up and said, "Yes, I would." So we knelt and prayed—and Tom asked Christ to come into his heart and save him. And he thanked God for loving him enough to die for him.

The next day Tom began reading the Bible. And every day he talked to God in prayer. And of course, he began to *know* the *love* of God. Tom grew to be a strong Christian, telling others about God's love. Tom *knew*—he had *experienced* it!

But even after we experience the love of God, it is something that we cannot fully grasp. It is so great—so completely inexhaustible. "That Christ may dwell in your hearts by faith; that ye, being rooted and grounded in love, May be able to comprehend with all saints what is the breadth, and length, and depth, and height; And to know the love of Christ, which passeth knowledge that ye might be filled with all the fulness of God" (Eph. 3:17-19).

When Nansen, the great explorer, tried to measure

the depth of the ocean in the far north, he used a long measuring line. When he discovered that he had not touched bottom, he wrote in his record, "Deeper than that." The next day he tried a longer line, only to write again, "Deeper than that." Several times more he tried but he did not reach the bottom. Finally he fastened all his lines together and let them down. But his last record was still like the first, "Deeper than that." He left without ever knowing the depth of the ocean at that particular point—except that it was deeper than so many thousands of feet.

It is much the same with God's love—the love that transcends all knowing. We may know how much a young child loves, or a growing son or daughter, or a brother or sister, or a husband or wife. We may understand the love of a parent for his children, or a patriot for his country, or a Christian for his Saviour. But in each case, the measuring line will be too short to measure God's love. And even if we were to add all these measurements together, we still could not begin to measure the love of Christ. At best, our knowledge is only partial. We can only say it is "Deeper than that."

The beloved Christian poetess, Annie Johnson Flint, has beautifully expressed the magnitude of God's love in the following lines:

How *broad* is His love? Oh, as broad as man's trespass,
As wide as the need of the world can be;
And yet to the need of one soul it can narrow,
He came to the world and He came to me.

How *long* is His love? Without end or beginning,
Eternal as Christ and His life it must be,
For to everlasting as from everlasting
He loveth the world and He loveth me.

How *deep* is His love? Oh, as deep as man's sinning,
As low as the uttermost vileness can be;
In the fathomless gulf of the Father's forsaking,
He died for the world and He died for me.

How *high* is His love? It is high as the heavens,
As high as the throne of His glory must be;
And yet from that height He has stooped to
redeem us,
He "so" loved the world and He "so" loved me.

How *great* is His love? Oh, it passes all knowledge,
No man's comprehension, its measure can be;
It filleth the world, yet each heart may contain it,
He "so" loved the world and He "so" loved me.

The greatness of God's love overwhelms us. Yet, there are some who dare to question His love.

"How can you believe in a God of love when there is so much suffering in the world?" You have heard people ask this. For some strange reason they blame God for everything that goes wrong in this sin-cursed world.

Dr. Richard Halverson, prominent Christian leader, tells of an incident that deals with this very thing. A godly pastor, recuperating from a siege of illness, sat in a wheel chair on the patio of the hospital. Another patient also in a wheelchair pointedly questioned him as to why God, if He loved people, would allow suffering. This woman had endured much pain and suffering, and her heart was bitter toward God.

"Do you believe in suffering?" asked the pastor.

"What do you mean by that?" the woman replied.

"Is suffering real?" continued the man. "Is suffering a fact?"

"IS IT A FACT!" she exclaimed angrily. "You don't spend three months in a hospital listening to the screams of women and children—seeing a woman brought into your ward one day, carried out under a sheet the next. You don't stay in a hospital as I have these past three months and have any doubt that suffering is real. Of course suffering is a fact!"

For thirty minutes the woman poured out the bitterness and cynicism that had soured in her spirit. True, her body had suffered much. And now her soul was suffering more.

"Very well, suffering is a fact. On this we agree," said the pastor. "Now try to explain this suffering without God. Does suffering make any more sense without believing in a God of love? Is suffering more bearable when you don't believe in Him?"

The woman was quiet for a long time. Slowly it dawned upon her that either consciously or unconsciously, the only thing that kept her sane through her intense physical suffering was the feeling that somehow, somewhere there was a God who cared, who loved, who understood. But overcome by self pity she had allowed bitterness to distort her reason and make her angry with God.

It may be difficult for finite human beings to explain how a God of love can allow the terrible agony and suffering and tragedy in the world. But it is infinitely more difficult to explain these tragic events by leaving God out of the picture. If there is no God that loves, then Shakespeare was right when he pessimistically described life as a "tale told by an idiot—full of sound and fury—signifying nothing . . ."

Suffering and tragedy remain. And there is no hope, no reason, no sense to life if man cannot count on a God who loves—and who can somehow in His providence turn tragedy into triumph! "Who shall separate us from the love of Christ? Shall tribulation, or distress, or persecution, or famine, or nakedness, or peril, or sword? . . . Nay, in all these things we are more than conquerors through Him that loved us (Rom. 8:35, 37).

God never leaves His redeemed in doubt as to His

love for them. He writes it on nearly every page of His Holy Word.

As we read the Bible He tells us that we are the object of His affection. On one page He says that He loves us. Then on the next He tells us again. Then again, and again. A wonderful story of love! He says, "... He that loveth me shall be loved of my Father, and I will love him and will manifest myself to him" (John 14:21).

This is in contrast to human love. People love in their limited way, and for a limited time. You can't always depend on human love, but you *can depend* on God's love. People may change their minds and turn against you—even forget you.

Dr. George Matheson was one of Scotland's ablest preachers and one of the world's greatest writers of devotional literature.

As a young man he was a student at the University of Glasgow. And it was then that he fell in love and was engaged to be married to a beautiful young Christian woman.

But before their wedding date, George Matheson became ill and the doctors told him that in time he would lose his eyesight. Immediately his mind turned to his sweetheart and his forthcoming marriage. He felt that it was his duty to write her and to tell her about the blindness which was coming over him. Hoping, of course, that she would not let him go, he offered to release her from the engagement.

When his sweetheart read the shocking news, she agreed that she would *not* want to go through life with a blind man. So she wrote him, stating that she would like to be released from the engagement.

This was a great blow to George Matheson. And after several years of severe mental suffering, he wrote the words to the immortal hymn, O LOVE THAT WILT NOT LET ME GO:

O Love that wilt not let me go,
I rest my weary soul in thee:
I give thee back the life I owe,
That in thine ocean depths its flow
May richer, fuller be.
O joy that seekest me through pain,
I cannot close my heart to thee;
I trace the rainbow through the rain,
And feel the promise is not vain
That morn shall tearless be.

On his way to happiness, George Matheson learned that human love is fragile, but that the love of God is endless and Divine!

3
The Guilt Complex

WITH ROGUISH grin and tongue in cheek, Sir Arthur Conan Doyle used to tell of a practical joke he played on his friends.

The story goes that he sent a telegram to twelve famous people, all of whom were men of great virtue and reputation and of considerable position in society. The message was worded, "Fly at once, all is discovered."

Within twenty-four hours all twelve of the so-called virtuous men had left the country!

Guilty conscience? Evidently! However, feelings of guilt are not limited to the famous. We *all* have them.

But the majority of us try to camouflage or rationalize our guilt. We excuse ourselves on the basis of being "better" than someone else. We "make up" for our guilt by doing kind and helpful deeds. Yet, mixed with these mental mechanisms are some troubled thoughts. Somehow we sense that such reasoning is flimsy and unsound. We strongly suspect that the guilt is still there.

RIGHT AND WRONG

This is a strange world—one filled with contrasts and incredible paradoxes. Light and dark, joy and sorrow, beauty and ugliness, love and hate, life and death—they are all here together and we accept them as a part of living. Conflict? Yes, constantly.

Looming up before us as one of the greatest of these conflicts stands *right* against *wrong*. Ever since the beginning of civilization when Adam and Eve used their free will to choose evil, it has always been *good* vs. *evil, innocence* vs. *guilt.* And because of man's nature, he has a bent toward sinning. Try as he might to do right, there is always *conscience*—condemning, pointing an accusing finger at every misdeed and inconsistency. And this insistent shadow haunts him day and night. The situation seems hopeless.

Yes, the situation *is* hopeless. And moreover, it is harmful. It is damaging to the human mind and body. Psychologists and psychiatrists know that a person cannot develop as he should if he harbors the feeling that he is guilty and sinful. It restricts and distorts his growth both emotionally and mentally. Since this is true, a sense of guilt is not a matter to be taken lightly.

Probably no one realizes better than those of us engaged in professional counseling, how really unique each person is. No two clients are alike. And yet, with all their differences they are much alike—especially in one way: at the core of most of their problems are feelings of guilt and sin.

Is it any wonder then, that in psychological circles, the "guilt complex" is a much *talked* about and much *written* about subject? Bookshelves and magazine racks are bulging with treatises and articles about the "guilt complex" and its detrimental effect on people. Naturally there are many solutions offered for resolving one's feelings of guilt. Because as psychologists and psychiatrists work with people they can see the trail of damage caused by guilt. They know it is a real menace.

A Universal Problem

It really doesn't matter on what part of the globe a person may live: if he is old enough to understand right and wrong, he realizes that he is guilty of sin. No, he may not want to admit it to you or anyone else. But deep down inside, if he's honest, he knows that all is not well.

Sin is a problem—a *real* problem—one that confronts the savage tribesman in Africa as well as the society belle in Hollywood. Here is a problem that must be dealt with by both the beggar in the alley and the millionaire on Wealthy Street. The guilt complex is "standard equipment" for all human beings. God says that "*all* have sinned and come short of the glory of God" (Rom. 3:23). And truly, man's conscience re-echoes the condemnation—"all have sinned."

I think of an experience in our own family. One evening not long ago, we sat listening to the radio as a mighty servant of God brought a challenging gospel message over the air. This particular night the subject was "The Fact of Sin." Evidently our little five year old daughter, Melodie, was impressed.

"Mommie," she said, looking up at my wife, "am *I* a sinner?"

"Yes, honey," my wife replied. "We are *all* sinners.

"You see," she continued to explain. "It is very easy for us to do naughty things. That's our nature. But we really have to *try* to be good."

Little Melodie sat quietly for a moment. Then she repeated thoughtfully, "Yes, that's right. It's *easy* to be naughty but it's *hard* to be good."

How true! There's not a person in the world who, if he is honest at all, cannot say the same thing.

The Consequences

What happens when we continually feel guilty? How does it affect our health and personality?

In the first place, a sense of guilt robs us of our happiness because it is a nagging reminder that we have not done the right thing. Happiness stems from inner satisfaction—a quality that disappears when guilt casts its dark shadow across our lives.

A guilt complex also shatters our confidence. When we look into our own lives, we see our imperfections. We know only too well what we are made of—what our inclinations are. The hope we once held for ourselves is gone. We are weak and we *know* it.

Guilt feelings remind us of the *past* and dim our *future*. Neither looks bright. Our past is marred by sin. And the future is but an extension of the past. When we look ahead our experience reminds us of what has happened before.

As it was with Adam and Eve in the garden of Eden, we, too, want to run away and hide from God—or to compensate for our wrongs. Sin never seeks the light. Sin is discouraging. It constantly reminds us that we are not worthy of love and respect.

The result?—we feel insecure. Our enthusiasm is dulled, and we become preoccupied with self rather than the challenging jobs at hand. We are not sure of ourselves because our conscience keeps hammering away—"guilty."

But that's not the only consequence of sin. Because we do not like to admit that we are sinners, we set up an emotional block against facing the facts—the facts that each of us is accountable to God and that God condemns us! We go through life trying to "prove" that we are all right when we know we are not.

It is little wonder then that people spend much time dodging serious thought about themselves and their sin. Some drink, some keep on the go, some occupy their minds with reading or viewing. Others search out entertainment—anything to avoid quiet times of serious reflection.

Humanity is *restless*. Searching—always searching but never finding that "something" which brings inner satisfaction and peace. People are troubled and uneasy. God Himself, knowing the nature of man, declares: "But the wicked are like the troubled sea, when it cannot rest, whose waters cast up mire and dirt. There is no peace, saith my God, to the wicked" (Isa. 57:20, 21).

Where Shall We Hide It?

"We must *do* something about this," insist psychologists and psychiatrists. "We must find ways to erase the guilt complex from people's minds."

So they devise various methods to assist people in "resolving" their guilt feelings.They have developed many ways to *rationalize* wrong doings and to discount sins as mere human "mistakes." They also lead their clients to think of sin as a behavior pattern which has not yet been incorporated into our society—frowned upon "here" but acceptable "there."

Sounds nice? Yes. The only trouble is that It Doesn't Work. Why? Because man does not have the power to remove sin. And the stark, grim reality is that no one is exempt: everyone *is* guilty.

But people do not like to admit guilt. That is why the world is filled with many methods of human justification. From the centers of advanced civilization to the most remote tribes of the world, people are busy with pseudo attempts to do away with guilt feelings. Some try to atone for their sins by inflicting bodily torture on themselves while others ease their conscience by donating to charity. But the principle is the same.

True, people can learn to *overlook* and *minimize* their guilt feelings. But they cannot eliminate sin. Oh yes, it may be possible to drive guilt feelings from a place of constant awareness, rationalize them to the point where they are not always confronting us. But in so doing, we drive them to a more damaging and subtle place—the subconscious. They are not eliminated at all: they are just planted a *little deeper*. And they will be sure to crop up again—more vigorous than ever. So it is that by merely painting over our sins, we do not eradicate them. In time, the paint will wear off.

Every man, woman and child who is honest with himself knows that he is not perfect. By nature and by choice he is a sinner. And it is the same the world over.

Deep down inside the heart of man, he realizes that he has missed the mark and is unfit to stand in the presence of perfection—a Holy God! And that, of course, is why he feels guilty.

A complex? Yes. But much more than that. People *feel guilty* because they *are guilty*.

Facing Reality

All children like to play "hide and seek." And our little daughter is no exception.

She does fairly well at it now—too well at times. But when she was younger, the game was quite amusing to us. For when it was her turn to hide, it made little difference to her if she were completely hidden or not. She seemed to think that as long as her face was hidden so that she could not see us, neither could we see *her*. Just like the proverbial ostrich burying his head in the sand.

Adults smile at this childish reasoning. But many times, we do no better in our reasoning about sin. How immature and childish we are to believe that just because we close our eyes and hide our faces from our sins, no one else sees them either. But even if we should camouflage our sins from the eyes of other people, God sees them all. We cannot hide from Him.

Think of it this way. Suppose we refuse to accept the fact that we have a serious illness. This does not make us well. To say we have no hideous malignancy when we know that it is viciously eating away at our very life is not to face the facts. And so it is with sin—ignoring it will by no means lessen its deadly consequences.

In the Bible God speaks simply and plainly of guilt and sin. He declares it to be a fact. In the Old Testament we read, "All we like sheep have gone astray; we have turned everyone to his own way, and the Lord hath laid on Him [Christ] the iniquity of us all" (Isa. 53:6). And in the New Testament God says, "For all have sinned and come short of the glory of God" (Rom. 3:23). "If we say that we have no sin, we deceive ourselves, and the truth is not in us" (I John 1:8).

Like others, I have read the writings of many men, but I have yet to find any scientific data that would even suggest that man has a perfect nature and is without sin. It is true that every person has innate ability—no doubt much more than he realizes. Yet, with all of his talents, he does have a sin problem that must be solved. To ignore this fact is pure folly—no matter how great our human potential may be.

But why do professional counselors such as psychologists and psychiatrists spend so much of the time trying to "resolve," "cover up," and "spell away" the guilt complex? Since sin is a reality, one wonders why they dodge the issue. Why don't they deal directly and practically with guilt and sin?

For years I have associated and worked with other professional counselors. The reason why my colleagues who are non-Christians will not look squarely at sin and deal with it directly is not difficult to understand. *Since they are not believers themselves, they have no spiritual insight.* People have spiritual understanding *only* when the Holy Spirit indwells them and guides their thinking. The Bible says, "But the natural man receiveth not the things of the spirit of God; for they are foolishness unto him; neither can he know them, because they are spiritually discerned" (I Cor. 2:14). This means the man in his natural (unsaved) condition can neither accept nor understand spiritual things because they are spiritually detected and understood. So naturally we cannot expect a professional counselor (regardless of his intellect or specialized training) to give godly advice if he does not have spiritual perception.

Not long ago I counseled with a man who had committed nearly every sin in the book. After paying out hundreds of dollars to unregenerate, professional counselors, he came to see me.

"I'm no better than I was when I first started receiving psychological help," he said.

And he was right. You see, he needed forgiveness—a clear conscience. And only God could give him that. So we settled it that day. He accepted Christ as his personal Saviour! Did he get relief? He surely did. Immediately his problem started clearing up.

Like this man, everyone needs to face facts. Sin is a *reality* and it must be dealt with in a *real* way.

THE REAL REMEDY

Guilt and sin are too big for man to cope with. But he doesn't need to. Christ has already paid the penalty for sin. With His great heart of love God opens His arms to us and says, "If we confess our sins, He is faithful and just to forgive us our sins, and to cleanse us from all unrighteousness" (I John 1:9).

Confess! This is the key.

Some time ago I talked with a well-educated man about his relationship to God. He was honest with himself and soon admitted that his own righteousness did not measure up to the standards of a holy God. For several weeks he read various portions of Scripture. And as he read, his heart and mind were touched by such verses as these: "Come now, and let us reason together, saith the Lord: though your sins be as scarlet, they shall be as white as snow; though they be red like crimson, they shall be as wool" (Isa. 1:18). "This is a faithful saying, and worthy of all acceptation, that Christ Jesus came into the world to save sinners; of whom I am chief" (I Tim. 1:15). "For God so loved the world, that he gave his only begotten Son, that whosoever believeth in him should not perish, but have everlasting life" (John 3:16).

A few weeks later this man told me that he wanted to accept Christ. We knelt quietly together and he opened his heart to Him and was truly saved. During the months that followed, he eagerly read God's Word and took part in Christian activities. My heart rejoiced as I saw him develop into a fine, mature Christian.

A few weeks later I had luncheon with a different man, also well educated. We discussed the Bible's concept of man and God's remedy for sin. When I had presented the thrilling story of God's plan of salvation, he looked at me and said, "I like the *love* part, Narramore, but the *damnation* part leaves me as cold as a clam. If I as a parent would not harm my child, why should God *harm* me? He's got us in a corner—He says 'Do what I say or I'll fry you in hell.' " Then with a look of arrogancy he added, "If I couldn't do a better job than God in making arrangements for love and rewards, I'd quit." This man, bitterly refusing the facts, rejected Christ and continued in his own, willful way.

Several years have passed. But I still see both of these men occasionally. They made their choices—and what a contrast! The first man is thrilled with life. The second is existing. One is realistically shaping the present and anticipating the future. The other is still betting on the human race, hoping that things will turn out all right sometime, somehow.

The first man, an outstanding educator, is leading others to Christ, while the second squirms any time God or death are discussed. The first man's family is following in his footsteps. The second man is leading his children into the dark with him.

The first man's basic psychological need—to be FREE FROM GUILT—has been met! As a child of God, he not only possesses eternal life, but he has forgiveness from sin. The second man is still attempting to rationalize his sin. He is struggling daily with a guilt complex—and fighting a losing battle.

The contrast between these two men started the day when each faced his accountability to God. One accepted it; the other rejected it. But whether we wish to acknowledge it or not, man is responsible to God not only after death, but during his life on earth.

It is evident that man is dependent upon God. Man did not create the world or the universe. God did. Man did not make himself. Neither did he give himself life. Man does not even provide the air which he breathes. Man is completely dependent on God and His creation. *Absolutely everything a person has is lent to him by God.* Man can lay claim to nothing. He is a user, an enjoyer of God's creation. But man himself cannot create anything independently. The songs he composes, the pictures he paints, the children he bears, even the steps he takes are the result of God having given him the necessary ability.

"But," you may say, "if man is accountable to God, doesn't this take away his free choice? Doesn't this make him a mechanical robot?"

No, because God *does* give man a mind, furnishing him with free choice. But *only in God's framework.* This is because God is infinite, but man is finite. Man must decide which road he will take. He must choose God or Satan—Heaven or Hell. He may think, "Why must I choose? I'll serve neither. I'll refuse both Heaven and Hell." But there is no neutral ground. Man can refuse God, but when he does, he is responsible for his own sin. He has made his choice. This means eternal separation from God.

Man's desire to set up his own terms is a clear revelation that he does not want to submit himself to God. And this rebellion is sin.

Can we trust and admire a God who controls the future? Yes! God is love. He is more concerned about our welfare than we are about our own. It was this divine concern that brought Christ to Calvary to make provision for our sin.

Freedom from guilt? Yes, God provides it be *removing our sin* from us. "As far as the east is from the west, so far hath he *removed* our transgressions from us" (Ps. 103:12).

A New Nature

An interesting story is told about a traveler in Italy who spent the night at a little wayside inn. The floor in his room was dreadfully dirty. He thought to himself, "I'll ask the landlady to scrub it." But when he saw that the floor was made of mud he gave it a second thought. *That won't do,* he mused. *The more she* scrubs, *the worse it will be.*

The same is true of man's nature. No amount of "fixing up" will change it. Trying to scrub away a person's guilt only shows up his sin to be blacker and muddier than ever. What he needs is a *new* nature. As God says, "You must be born again" (John 3:7). Then, and *only* then, can he have a new nature.

"How can a man be born when he is old?"

This is a legitimate question. Nicodemus asked the same thing. But Jesus had the answer!

First He made it clear that the new birth is a mystery. The wind blows where it wills, and you hear the sound, but you do not know whence it comes or whither it goes; so it is with every one who is born of the Spirit" (John 3:8).

This does not mean it is irrational . . . it is supra-rational. It is the WORK OF GOD and therefore outside man's intellectual comprehension. And even though the new birth cannot be explained, it can be experienced! You may not know where the wind comes from or where it's going—but you know it's blowing. So it is that a man can be born again without knowing how it works.

What does a person do to be born of God? Jesus said simply, "Come unto Me . . ." And anyone who responds to His simple invitation will be met by God. The new birth is not something one can do for himself. It is not a human invention. It is the work of God alone! God will do this for any man who desires it. The only requirement for the new birth is *willingness.*

So when a person admits his guilt, asks forgiveness for his sins, and invites Christ into his heart, God meets him with the gift of a new spiritual life—a nature that is God-like rather than sinful. "But as many as received Him, to them gave He power to become the sons of God, even to them that believe on His name: Which were born, not . . . of the flesh, nor of the will of man, but of God" (John 1:12, 13).

With sins forgiven and with a new nature, the guilt complex doesn't stand a chance. It goes out when the guilt is removed. "Therefore if any man be in Christ, he is a new creature: old things are passed away; behold, all things are become new" (II Cor. 5:17).

Gone Forever

Life offers no joy that compares with the realization of sins forgiven. The past and present are as white as snow. This is our condition when we accept Christ.

Satan doesn't give up that easily, however. Although he has lost the battle for an eternal soul, he continually tempts the Christian with, "Are your sins *really* forgiven—*all* of them?"

These questions remind me of Joe. We were graduate students together at Columbia University; he in the field of science and I in education and psychology. Then one day I had the privilege of leading Joe to the Lord. Immediately we set up a program of study and memorization of the Word.

A couple of weeks passed. Then one day when we saw each other in the library he said, "Narramore, are you sure *all* my sins are forgiven?"

"Why do you ask?"

"Don't get me wrong. I'm saved, and I know it. But last night I got to thinking about some of the things I had done in the past. As I thought about them I wondered, 'Can it be that God has forgiven me of *all* those sins?' "

"Yes, Joe," I said. "There's nothing you can think

of that He hasn't forgiven. But come, sit down. Let's get God's own assurance."

As we sat there together we turned to Isaiah 1:18, "Come now, and let us reason together, saith the Lord: though your sins be as scarlet, they shall be as white as snow; though they be red like crimson, they shall be as wool." Next we looked at I John 1:9, "If we confess our sins, He is faithful and just to forgive us our sins, and to cleanse us from all unrighteousness."

"How much sin is He able to cleanse us from, Joe?"

"*All* unrighteousness."

"Who says so?"

"God."

"Can God lie?"

"No, never!"

"Then, on the basis of the fact that you have accepted Christ as your own personal Saviour, and have asked Him to forgive your sins, has He forgiven you of *all* your past sin?"

Joe looked up from The Book and with tears in his eyes said, "Praise God! They're *all* forgiven!"

Satan never tempted Joe again about his past sins. Joe had God's Word for it and he knew it was settled —*forever.*

How about you? Has Satan been tempting you with the thought that perhaps not all your sins were forgiven the day you gave your heart to Christ? That is a trick he often pulls. You see, if he can get you to believe that lie, he will rob you of your joy and he will cripple your testimony.

If you are a believer, your sins are forgiven! It makes no difference whether you feel it or not—it does not change the facts. You may *think* your sins are not forgiven, but God says they are forgiven. So they are.

Not long ago a lady from the midwest wrote me a letter saying that although she was born-again and daily asked forgiveness of sin, a wrong she had done many years ago was still tormenting her. I wrote this dear lady, giving her the same Scriptures I had given Joe several years before. I also suggested that she read the Fifty-first Psalm several times. Then I pointed out that no matter what she *thought* about her past sins, she couldn't possibly change the fact that they *were* forgiven.

"It's your feelings over against God's Word," I added. "Wouldn't you prefer to believe God?"

When the lady really believed God, she soon had victory over this concern and ceased her doubting.

You see, if human beings did the "forgiving" we couldn't be so sure that they would "stay" forgiven. But because of the life and death and resurrection of Christ, we are assured of God's complete forgiveness for *all* our sin. We are free from all guilt. Past, present and future! But to experience God's *daily forgiveness* we need only to confess our daily sins, then we have complete forgiveness. Naturally, we must do this as soon as we are aware of any sin in our lives. "And if any man sin, we have an advocate with the Father, Jesus Christ the righteous" (I John 2:1).

As children of God we are not to be satisfied with sin in our lives. If we find that we are doing things which are contrary to the Bible and the will of God, we will not want to continue doing them because we love Christ. "He that hath my commandments, and keepeth them, he it is that loveth me: and he that loveth me shall be loved of my Father, and I will love him and will manifest myself to him" (John 14:21).

There is nothing more basic to happiness than peace of mind. But it is ours only as we are free from guilt. There is no solution other than salvation. And when we know Christ, we have the assurance that our sins are gone forever and that we can have cleansing for our daily walk. This brings complete freedom from guilt. This is THE WAY TO HAPPINESS!

4
Belonging

SOME YEARS AGO the *New York Times* printed a human interest story entitled, "He Would Like to Belong." The article told about a small boy who was riding on a downtown bus. There he sat, huddled close to a lady in a gray suit. Naturally, everyone thought he belonged to her. Little wonder, then, that when he rubbed his dirty shoes against a woman sitting on the other side of him, she said to the lady in the gray suit, "Pardon me, but would you please make your little boy take his feet off the seat? His shoes are getting my dress dirty."

The woman in gray blushed. Then giving the boy a little shove, she said, "He's not *my* boy. I never saw him before."

The lad squirmed uneasily. He was such a tiny little fellow, his feet dangling off the seat. He lowered his eyes and tried desperately to hold back a sob.

"I'm sorry I got your dress dirty," he said to the woman. "I didn't mean to."

"Oh, that's all right," she answered, a little embarrassed. Then, since his eyes were still fastened upon her, she added, "Are you going somewhere—*alone*?"

"Yes," he nodded, "I always go alone. There isn't anyone to go with me. I don't have any mommie or daddy. They're both dead. I live with Aunt Clara but she says Aunt Mildred ought to help take care of me part of the time. So when she gets tired of me and wants to go some place, she sends me over to stay with Aunt Mildred."

"Oh," said the woman, "are you on your way to Aunt Mildred's now?"

"Yes," the boy continued, "but sometimes Aunt Mildred isn't home. I sure hope she's there today because it looks like it's gonna rain and I don't want to be out in the street when it rains."

The woman felt a little lump in her throat as she said, "You've a very little boy to be shifted around like this."

"Oh, I don't mind," he said. "I never get lost. But I get lonesome sometimes. So when I see someone that I think I would like to belong it, I sit real close and snuggle up and pretend I really do belong to them. I was playing that I belonged to this other lady when I got your dress dirty. I forgot about my feet."

The woman put her arms around the little fellow and "snuggled" him up so close that it almost hurt. He wanted to belong to someone. And deep in her heart she wished that he belonged to her.

This little boy, in his artless, childlike fashion, had expressed a universal need. And it does not matter who he is or how old he is: *everyone wants to belong.*

The Desire to Belong

"It is not good that the man should be alone."

God spoke these words at the very beginning of human history. You remember the story—how God created the first man, Adam, and then, because man needed companionship, God created Eve, the first woman.

"And the Lord God said, It is not good that the man should be alone. I will make an help meet for him" (Gen. 2:18).

This desire to be with others is innate. It is a "built-in" psychological need placed there by God. We see its evidence on every hand. People cling together as families, they cluster together in communities and towns and cities, they give their allegiance to their country and even sacrifice their lives to preserve its unity. A "man without a country" is a pathetic case; and the man, woman, or child without a family, or without friends, is the object of sympathy. There is no one to whom he belongs.

People need each other and want to "belong." Many are concerned about getting married because they do not want to live alone. We all like to feel that we are related in some way to others and that we are part of a group. We feel secure when we think that we are included and we are happy when our interests and feelings are shared by others. So we form countless organizations and clubs for people to join. There are societies, brotherhoods, lodges, sororities, fraternities, leagues, unions, trusts, fellowships, gangs and guilds. They are service clubs, hobby groups, sports clubs, professional groups, cultural societies, religious groups, and political organizations. We find clubs for tall people, clubs for short people, clubs for single people, clubs for married people, clubs for young, clubs for old, clubs for everyone. These efforts on the part of man to form into groups are merely further indications of his basic psychological need—that of *belonging*.

Yes, all normal people like to *belong*. It is a God-given desire—and it is a satisfying experience.

When You Don't Belong

But what about the person who feels that he just does *not* belong—he would rather be by himself? Is this a wholesome attitude?

No, and this is usually a serious symptom. Because it is a psychological fact that we are social beings and we need social relationships if we are to maintain good mental health.

The person who is a "lone wolf" cannot adjust to society. It is abnormal for people to want to be alone. Naturally, everyone needs to be alone *part* of the time —but always to prefer your own company to that of other human beings is not a healthy attitude. The proverbial hermit who lives alone in an isolated shack is tabbed "peculiar"—and of course, he is. When a person loses contact with others and cannot fit into a desirable social pattern it is a danger signal. Psychiatric social workers look upon "aloneness" as an unhealthy sign.

School psychologists are constantly on the alert for children who are isolates, boys and girls who are always on the outer edge of activities. They know that such tendencies in childhood often lead to real trouble later on. If these children are spotted, they can be helped to fit into groups situations and thereby develop into normal, healthy members of society.

How does it feel to *not* belong?

Here is the answer in the words of thousands of people who experience it, "No one wants me." I'm not good enough for them." "I can't please anyone." "No one cares and there's no use trying." "There must be something wrong with me." "No one understands, and I'm all by myself."

It is not a comfortable feeling, is it?—always to be left out, standing back along the fringes and never finding your way into the center. It's lonely; it's desolate.

This barren, rejected feeling can gradually push a person closer to a serious breakdown. Psychologists and psychiatrists find that many of their clients have long histories of not belonging.

How well I remember a woman who suffered from this very thing—she never belonged. True, she had tried desperately to be accepted by others; she had joined nearly every club in town. Oh yes, she attended the meetings, paid the dues, and went out of her way to get into the whirl of things. But still she was never really one of them. She didn't seem to fit. In time this "left out" feeling caught up with her in the form of physical aches and pains.

People feel it keenly when they think no one wants or understands them. It is not enough to say that those who are overwhelmed by "aloneness" do not develop fully. Frustration caused by this unmet need can lead to severe psychopathology. Indeed, this unmet need is the cause of various neurotic symptoms—many of which can become very serious. Excessive daydreaming, stuttering, loss of appetite, depression, and various forms of obsession—these and other symptoms often develop when people continually feel rejected or isolated. Some people actually develop stomach ailments, palpitations of the heart, and muscular aches and pains without knowing what caused them.

During the recent World War, I had an experience which I shall always remember. While serving as a naval officer I was sent to a small island in the North Atlantic, the country of Iceland. There, stretched across the bleak, desolate lava fields not far from the Arctic Circle, lay the Keflavik Air Base. The winter was dreary and dark. The long nights stretched into the days, crowding out the sunlight. Life for the most part was dull and lonely. Apart from the Air Base there were no houses, no trees, no vegetation—just endless nothingness. To our boys in blue and khaki the culture of the people was different. The harsh, Viking tongue was different. The cold, arctic climate was different. Everything was strange and different.

Many of our American boys found that psychologically they couldn't take it. Shortly before I arrived, ships sailed back across the North Atlantic to the United States, carrying a large number of American military personnel who were forced to leave because of poor mental health. For the most part, their mental illnesses were attributed to the fact that these men could not adjust to the strangeness of that land. Life there seemed so remote—so different from anything they had ever known. Familiar sights were missing, the countryside was barren and forbidding, and the language seemed impossible to learn. In the lives of these men, one thing was apparent: *they did not belong*. The basic need of "belonging" was not being met in their lives and the result was an emotional breakdown serious enough to send them home.

Not to "belong" usually leads to trouble. We cannot ignore this psychological need without reaping the consequences.

Helping Others Belong

What makes you like your closest friend? Is it wealth? Looks? Education? Fame? No, none of these. True friendship hinges on something much more basic and important. You like your friends because they make you feel comfortable. They appreciate you. You feel that when you are around them, *you belong.*

And just as you enjoy having others make you feel that *you* belong, so others appreciate your making them feel that *they* belong.

One of the secrets of happiness is to invest yourself in others—to use every opportunity to make them feel wanted.

The techniques for helping people feel that they belong are sometimes subtle. It is so easy to unwittingly make people feel that they do not belong. The thoughtful person is alert to the things he should avoid.

(1) *Undue or continual criticism.* This is one of the most effective ways to make a person feel that he does not belong. Criticism tells a person, "We don't like the way you do things and we would be happier if you weren't around." Criticism sets up a barrier between ourselves and the other person and he feels that we are not pleased with him.

(2) *Unfavorable comparisons.* These have much the same effect as criticism. We seldom solve people's problems by comparing one person unfavorably with another. Parents and teachers especially need to guard against this. Unfavorable comparisons do three things: They cause us to dislike the one with whom we are compared; they cause us to resent the one who did the

comparing; and they make us dislike the place where it occurred.

(3) *Assigning unsuitable tasks.* When people are given jobs which they do not understand or which they find too difficult, they become embarrassed. They feel that they have lost "prestige." They think that others must hold it against them because they were not able to come through with the expected results.

(4) *Thoughtless teasing or embarrassment.* Whether the "remark" is about clothing, mannerisms, speech, finances, appearance, accomplishments, friends, or ideas, the result is much the same. A person feels, "I don't suit them: I just don't fit in here."

(5) *Taking a person for granted.* Failure to recognize one's contribution and accomplishments makes him feel that you do not appreciate him and that you do not accept him. In whose progress are most people interested? Their own, of course. So when we ignore other people's efforts, we tell them, in a sense, that we are not interested in them.

These are practical, everyday concerns—and not one of us can afford to overlook them! In our homes, churches, schools, communities and various other organizations we have a responsibility to encourage and help those about us. This brings happiness to others, but it brings even more to *us*!

Today's alert classroom teachers are beginning to take special note of children who do not seem to belong. Through sociometric techniques, classroom teachers are learning to identify boys and girls who are not chosen or who are avoided by others. Misfits? Perhaps, but the teacher knows that these youngsters may be heading toward serious maladjustments unless steps are taken to help them.

Of the more than one million juvenile delinquents in America this year, most of them feel that they are not really wanted! No one knows exactly how many boys and girls in the United States run away from home, "floating" from one section of the country to another. But the California Director of Youth Authority says that in the State of California alone, two thousand youngsters escape to his state *every month.* Law enforcement agencies declare that without exception these young people are convinced that they do not belong.

Parents have a special responsibility. When children feel that they are "rejected," they usually resort to undesirable behavior in order to gain some recognition. Strange? No, belongingness is such a basic need that it must be met, either acceptably or unacceptably.

As I counsel with people I find that many marriage problems stem from this basic cause—a husband or wife does not feel that he or she is wholeheartedly accepted by his mate. The Miltons were an example of this. When they came to my office they were on the verge of separation. As I worked through on the case I found that the husband spent most of his time criticizing his wife. Did he love her? Yes, but because he constantly found fault, his wife felt as though she could never do anything to please him. Day by day the husband destroyed his wife's feeling of belonging to him.

"I think," she said, "that we would both be happier without each other." Actually Mr. Milton did not realize how rejected he was making his wife feel.

"Belongingness"—yes, it is a basic psychological need that must be met in the lives of people of every age—including those who are *older*. How much healthier and happier our grandparents would be if they were made to feel that they were wanted, loved, needed and appreciated.

The same thing is true with all our relationships in life. Whether it is at home, at school, on the job, or at church—we can and should make other people feel that they belong.

This is a challenge. And a serious responsibility. Our cues, then, are: compliment, notice, listen, appreciate, encourage and cooperate—the cues for happy and useful living.

Belonging to God

"It's mine," the boy said, holding his little boat with loving satisfaction and pride. "I *made* it myself!"

There was no question about it. He had made it for himself—for his own enjoyment. The boat *belonged* to him.

And so it is with God. He created man for Himself—for His own pleasure. "Thou has created all things, and for thy pleasure they are and were created" (Rev. 4:11).

Although God created people for each other (ordaining marriage, blessing the home, and sanctioning human government), His primary purpose in creating human beings was for fellowship with Himself. "And God said, Let us make man in our image, after our likeness . . . So God created man in his own image, in the image of God created he him; male and female created he them" (Gen. 1:26, 27). Rightfully then, man belonged to God because He *made* him.

Belonging to God! What could be more complete; what could be more satisfying? Man enjoyed a perfect bond of fellowship with God, his Creator—*until man wilfully broke this relationship by sinning.*

After that, everything was changed. Man had given himself over to Satan and was now controlled by sin. His nature was sinful and he was alienated from God. "Your iniquities have separated between you and your God, and your sins have hid His face from you, that He will not hear" (Isa. 59:2). Man no longer belonged to God: he was now "of his father, the devil" (John 8:44). A severe statement? Indeed. But also a very severe *fact.*

Could any tragedy be greater—to be estranged from the One who made us for Himself? Separated from God—here, during our life span on earth, and for eternity. How it must grieve the heart of God. And what a complete void is left in the heart of man. For although people can and should belong to one another, they were created as spiritual beings. They *need* to belong to God.

God knows this. And He wants us to belong to Him. Although mankind has chosen *not* to belong to God, in His divine love and tender compassion, He has chosen us. "Ye have not chosen me, but I have chosen you" (John 15:16). The great heart of God has provided a way that makes it possible for us to *belong* to Him—now and forever. But we must *accept* His provision.

What is this provision? It is God's own beloved Son, Jesus Christ. "For there is one God, and one mediator between God and men, the man Christ Jesus" (I Tim. 2:5). "But now in Christ Jesus ye who sometimes were far off are made nigh by the blood of Christ" (Eph. 2:13).

The boy who held his little boat and said, "It's mine, I made it," suffered a keen disappointment. One day, with exuberant anticipation he carried his boat to the shore of the lake and sailed it on the clear, blue water. The little boat skimmed along as the gentle breeze blew its sails across the rippling waves. Then suddenly a gust of wind caught the little boat and snapped the string the boy was holding. On, on—out further and further the little boat sailed until at last it had vanished from sight.

Sadly the boy made his way home—without his prized possession. It was lost.

The weeks and the months went by. Then one day as the boy passed by a toy shop, something caught his attention. Could it be? Was it really? He looked closer. *It was.* Yes, there in the display window was his *own* little boat.

Overjoyed, the boy bolted into the store and told the owner about the boat on display. It really belonged to him. He had *made* it, hadn't he?

"I'm sorry," the shopkeeper said, "but it's *my* boat now. If you want it, you'll have to pay the price for it."

Sad at heart, the boy left the store. But he was determined to get his boat back, even though it meant working and saving until he had enough money to pay for it.

At last the day came. Clutching his money in his fist, he walked into the shop and spread his hard earned money on the counter top. "I've come to buy back my boat," the boy said.

The clerk counted the money. It was enough. Reaching into the showcase, the storekeeper took the boat and handed it to the eager boy.

The lad's face lit up with a smile of satisfaction as he held the little boat in his arms. "You're mine," he said, "*twice* mine. Mine because I *made* you—and now, mine because I *bought* you."

So it is with our relationship to God. We are His twice. His first because He made us. Then because we turned away from Him, Satan took over. "All we like sheep have gone astray; we have turned everyone to his own way" (Isa. 53:6). But God wanted us so greatly that He paid the price to buy us back. The price was tremendous—the highest price that ever could be paid. It was the sacrifice of His own Son, Jesus, upon the Cross of Calvary. "Forasmuch as ye know that ye were not redeemed with corruptible things, as silver and gold . . . But with the precious blood of Christ, as of a lamb without blemish and without spot" (I Peter 1:18, 19).

Think of it. God paid the price of sin through the shed blood of His own Son so that He might *buy us back*—redeem us. And because of this, *we can belong to Him*. Today. Tomorrow. Throughout eternity.

It is an overwhelming thought when we consider the close, intimate relationship which God provides for those who accept Christ as their personal Saviour! In this wonderful relationship with God, we are His *sons*

—His very own. "Beloved, now are we the sons of God, and it doth not yet appear what we shall be: but we know that, when He shall appear, we shall be like him; for we shall see him as He is" (I John 3:2). What could be closer! What could be sweeter! We belong now because we are "*accepted* in the beloved" (Eph. 1:6).

God reminds us that He is the vine and we are the branches (John 15:5). In other words, our relationship with Him is so close that it would be impossible to remove one without taking part of the other. He also tells us that He is our shepherd. But most intimate of all is the fact that we are actually *indwelt by God's Holy Spirit!* "Know ye not that ye are the temple of God, and that the Spirit of God dwelleth in you?" (I Cor. 3:16).

When we belong to God, He promises that He will never leave us nor forsake us. Man may be fickle, but God is sure. He is steadfast. And when we belong to Him we can say with the Apostle Paul, "For I am persuaded that neither death, nor life, nor angels, nor principalities, nor powers, nor things present, nor things to come, Nor height, nor depth, nor any other creature, shall be able to separate us from the love of God, which is in Christ Jesus our Lord" (Rom. 8:38, 39). Could any "belonging" be more satisfying than this?

Truly, when we belong to God we have His fellowship and His companionship. Nothing can meet man's need for belonging in any fuller or richer degree. The Irishman expressed it well when he and his Christian friend were talking.

"It's a grand thing to be saved," the friend said.

"Aye," answered the Irishman, "it is. But I know something better than that."

"Better than being saved?" the other asked in surprise. "What can possibly be better than that?"

"The companionship of the One who has saved me," was the reply.

There is nothing sweeter. Fellowship with God exceeds all other joy here on earth or in heaven. And is ours to enjoy forever.

Belonging to God's Family

Whenever I travel throughout the United States or in foreign countries, one significant fact always stands out: there is a close-knit bond of fellowship among true believers that exists in no other area of society. It is a *kinship* of one Christian to another. They all belong to the redeemed family of God.

Even though they may be complete strangers, when a child of God meets another of "like precious faith," they feel a oneness and a genuine warmth. They have much in common. They *belong*. The closeness they feel is not only because they share similar experiences, but because the same God, in the person of the Holy Spirit, indwells each of them. In other words, they are "spiritual relatives"—God is their Father and they are "brothers" or "sisters" in Christ. And this tie is far stronger than any human tie could possibly be: it is a relationship that will last for eternity.

Two brothers were traveling together in Europe. One was a Christian but the other was not. The unconverted brother was a member of the Masonic Lodge.

Like most Americans, they were always on the lookout for other U. S. citizens. So when they heard that there was an American in the town where they were staying, they visited him and learned that he was a gospel missionary. Immediately the two Christians began talking about the blessings of the Lord. What a time of fellowship! After a short visit the brothers went on their way.

They had no sooner stepped into the street when the Mason said to his brother, "Say, I didn't know you knew him before. When had you met him?"

"Never saw him before in my life," answered the Christian.

"What!" exclaimed the brother.

"That's right."

"Well, I've never seen the like. You never saw him before and yet for the last hour you've been talking like long lost friends."

"That's because we both know the Lord," the Christian replied. "We are brothers in Christ."

The Mason was silent. Then a moment later he added thoughtfully, "Well, John, I must admit, this sure beats Masonry."

And he was right. The bond of Christian fellowship surpasses all other human bonds. God speaks of this relationship (that of one Christian to another) as being parts of one body—His Church. Nothing can be in closer harmony than the parts of the body. They work together with minutest precision, they cooperate with each other, they "sympathize" with each other. In short, they operate as one because they *belong* together. And Christians belong together because they are *in Christ.*

During the last World War, a report from China told of a Japanese soldier who entered a Chinese Christian church at service time. His entrance created considerable apprehension and alarm until he stood up and said, "I am a conscript soldier, but I am also a Christian. If I may, I would like to worship with you."

The congregation breathed easily once again. Of course he was welcomed.

At the close of the service the Japanese soldier shook hands with the Chinese minister and asked him to sign his Bible.

The pastor gladly obliged. And beneath his signature he wrote in Chinese, "There is neither Jew nor Greek, there is neither bond nor free . . . for ye are all one in Christ Jesus" (Gal. 3:28).

How true! Neither Jew nor Greek; neither Chinese nor Japanese, nor American, nor any other earthly division—in Christ. There are no barriers of language or birth when we are children of the King. We are all "one in Christ Jesus." The poet expresses it beautifully in the following lines:

In Christ there is no East or West,
In Him no South or North;
But one great fellowship of love,
To show His glories forth.
In Him do true hearts everywhere
This sweet communion find;
His service we do gladly share
In love to all mankind.

Join hands then, brothers of the faith,
Whate'er your race may be:
Each one who loves the blessed Lord
Shares in His victory.
In Christ now meet both East and West,
In Him meet South and North:
All blood-bo't souls are in Him blest,
Thro' them his love flows forth.
—*J. Oxenham*

What is the tie that binds our hearts together in Christian love and unity? What is the basis of our fellowship? God gives the answer in His Word; "But if we walk in the light, as He is in the light, we have fellowship one with another, and the blood of Jesus Christ His Son cleanseth us from all sin" (I John 1:7). That's it. We must *walk* in the light—the Christian walk. Then it is that we have fellowship "one with another." Then it is that we sense our state of belonging—"one with another."

Belonging. How well I remember my own experience in Iceland. Just shortly before I arrived there as an officer in the Navy, a shipload of military personnel was transported back to the States because those men did *not* belong. The mental strain had been too much.

Now I was to be stationed there. But I wasn't alone. God, my Father, was with me. Soon I discovered that many of God's people were there. And although the country was different, the climate was different, the language was different—our God was the same. And I *belonged*.

I had only been there a few days when someone knocked at the door of my quonset hut. I opened the door and before me stood two fair complexioned young men—typical Icelanders. They smiled and cordially introduced themselves as Christians. A friend from the States, Krist Gudnason, had written about my coming to Iceland.

This was the beginning of a blessed time for me. It wasn't long before these two friends introduced me to many more Christians. I attended church with them and visited their homes. We spent many happy hours together—hours that were a spiritual blessing and an inspiration to me. Our bonds in Christ became so strong that when my tour of duty in that country came to an end, it was with reluctance that I said "goodbye" to my many Icelandic Christian friends.

As I left that little land that I had come to love and appreciate, I thought of the contrast between my tour of duty there and that of my fellow service men. They were shipped home for treatment and observation because they could not belong.

Indeed, man's need for belonging is best met in the Christian life. Because Christ has redeemed us by His blood, we belong to God. This is the ultimate in belonging. Nothing can exceed the satisfaction of knowing that God is our Father and we are His children—the object of His love and care.

And when we belong to God, we belong to each other—*in Christ*. This is the key to genuine fellowship. It unlocks the hearts of true believers around the world—and causes us to *belong*. Such belonging is not only human: it is divine. For when we belong to God's family, the relationship never changes—and we belong forever!

5

Knowledge That Satisfies

THERE HE LAY—just a tiny, sweet bundle of babyhood as he trustingly looked up into his mother's face. The age of innocence? Ah yes, but more than that. He was completely uninformed. You see, tiny Tommy hadn't lived long—*and he had a lot to learn.*

But it didn't take him long to start learning. And once he began, there was no stopping him for the rest of his life. Tommy soon learned that when he cried, he got attention. And as time went on, he learned new and better ways of expressing himself. He learned about this strange and wonderful world in which he lived: about people and plants and water and weather and animals and ants—yes, about *all sorts of things.*

But interestingly enough, the more Tommy learned, the more he wanted to learn. And the more he studied, the more he began to realize how much there was to learn, and how little he really knew. Tommy went through elementary school, then high school—and college. But he never finished learning.

Was Tommy an exception? No, not at all. People are made like that. It's human nature to want to learn and gain knowledge. Like Tommy, every individual starts from "scratch." And like Tommy, the desire to learn, understand and gain knowledge is one that will continue as long as he lives. Why? Because it is one of man's basic psychological needs—an "inner hunger." Truly, we are *born to learn.*

That is why every normal person wants to learn. And why the happiest and healthiest people are those who have an opportunity to satisfy their God-given curiosity.

Naturally we do not all seek the same information. The interests of the bank clerk may differ widely from that of the circus acrobat. And the primitive tribesman does not search for knowledge in the same way the atomic scientist does. Nevertheless, everyone wants to learn the things that seem important to him.

This basic psychological need, the desire to learn and gain knowledge, is one of the primary characteristics that distinguishes man from the animal kingdom. Here is a quality that sets him apart from other forms of life. Animals don't crave education. In fact, they resist it. Most animal trainers use one of two methods to persuade animals to learn their routines—sugar or the whip. But not so with people. With them the incentive is knowledge itself. And people will go to all extremes in order to learn, to develop intellectually. God created man to think, to perceive, to make decisions, and man is not happy unless he is learning.

Is it surprising then, that your personality develops as you learn? Those who want education but who have never had the opportunity to get it are often frustrated. Other things being equal, when you have had the opportunity to investigate and acquaint yourself with facts, you are more interesting. You have a finer personality and you can better face the demands of life.

Learning Is Big Business

Not long ago an elderly man with whom I was counseling told me, "Dr. Narramore, if I had it to do over again, I would get more education."

As he spoke, his voice carried a tone of regret. Actually, this man echoed the thoughts of thousands of his fellow men. People are seldom satisfied with what they know. They want to know more—and more—and when they have learned more, their thirst for knowledge is still not quenched.

That is why learning has become such important business—BIG BUSINESS. In our civilized world education is a giant concern of man. Various schools are open "around the clock." Day schools, night schools, colleges, universities, institutes, summer schools, correspondence schools, trade schools, nursery schools, graduate schools—yes, schools and courses that fit every age and need. But schools are not all. The printed page fills men's eyes and minds with facts, figures and fancies. Books, magazines, newspapers and literature of every description fly off the presses by the millions. What a tremendous effort people make to meet this inner hunger in their lives—the basic psychological need of inquiring and gaining knowledge!

A few years ago while I was in New York I was invited to speak at a banquet in the Hotel Astor. For my speech I wanted to know the number of books and periodicals published each year in the United States. So I phoned some of the so-called authorities. But no one knew the answer.

Finally, I went to the well known source of authority, the radio "Answer Man," who answers questions on every subject. But after talking to several of his secretaries, and finally getting through to the "Answer Man" himself, I learned that this time I had stumped the "Answer Man." Not even *he* knew how many books and periodicals were published each year.

But he *did* give me some sources that I could contact in order to come up with my own findings.

By contacting the publishers and other sources suggested, and by adding the various figures, I arrived at the staggering answer. I found that if all the books and periodicals published in the United States in one year were placed on top of each other, and if they were each an inch thick (many are more than that), they would reach up to the top of the Empire State Building which is 102 stories high—not just once or twice but 3,200 times! In other words, stacked skyward, these books would make 3,200 piles, each as high as the Empire State Building.

My mind was running rampant now, stimulated by the overwhelming mountain of books published annually—so I sharpened my pencil again. This time I discovered that if these books were all placed end to end they would extend far enough to build a causeway across the ocean to Paris—and then back again to New York. And what's more, there would be enough books left over to reach all the way from New York to Chicago.

Reading material? Miles and miles of it. Books written on every subject imaginable. But with all of this, we still want to learn more. And we always will. Solomon wasn't exaggerating when he said, ". . . of making many books there is no end . . ." (Eccl. 12:12).

Today, more than ever, people feel the need for knowledge. Because of widespread educational opportunities, radios, television, literature and other means of communication, in all probability people possess more information than they have in any other generation in the history of mankind. But are they content with this vast store of knowledge? Hardly! For there is always more to learn—and people are always craving to know it.

So it is that the business of *learning* truly is BIG BUSINESS. And, as the British writer, Lawrence Sterne, has expressed it, "the desire of knowledge, like the thirst of riches, increases ever with the acquisition of it!" Who can deny this?

INCENTIVES

In today's world ignorance is *not* bliss—it is a decided handicap. And those who could climb to the top must have something to offer: either knowledge or skill. A few of the incentives that spur us on to get more education are quite obvious, while others are more subtle.

Some people travel the path of knowledge believing

that it will eventually lead to happiness. They feel that if they learn more, their lives will be enriched and they will have more capacity for enjoyment. In a sense, this is true. For we *do* improve our personalities and gain self-confidence and poise as we become better informed.

Others pursue education and training because they believe that they have *unusual gifts or talents* which deserve to be developed. Singer, artist, playwright, or salesman—a man's innate ability needs polishing and refining if it is to be a scintillating jewel instead of a rough piece of rock. Talent isn't enough. It takes a lot of ambition and good solid training to bring out its luster.

In most cases, those who have more education and training get the *better jobs*. Advanced degrees usually demand bigger pay-checks. A real premium is placed upon knowledge, giving its owner a distinct advantage in life. Many times it is the password that permits a person to start on the road to success. So people are willing to sacrifice if necessary, in order to obtain the education that will eventually afford a *higher standard of living*.

Then there are some who are spurred on to higher learning because they want prestige—the *admiration* of their fellow men. They realize that recognition and acclaim usually go to those who have more knowledge.

Still others seek knowledge because they believe it is the key to *freedom*. And it is true that when people have the facts, they can make wiser choices. Education and Democracy have always been allies—while on the other side of the wall, bondage and ignorance go hand in hand.

There are people who know that knowledge is a source of *power*. Power to control, force and sway. This authority complex rules them until they rule others.

Some men realize that if they are to make any

contribution in life, they must know something. Effectiveness and ignorance are not compatible. And people want and need to feel that they are useful, that their service in life is fruitful. Henry Ford, the great industrialist, once said, "Anyone who stops learning is old whether this happens at twenty or eighty. Anyone who keeps on learning not only remains young but becomes constantly more valuable, regardless of physical capacity."

But that's not all. Among the millions of inhabitants of the earth, many seek knowledge with a much deeper motive than any of the ones discussed. People are looking for the "*why* of life." Just what is man's role upon earth? Why did God put us here? Is there any purpose in life? With these vital questions still unanswered they enter erudite halls of learning in search of "truth" that will answer the riddle of life.

Helping Others

We need not study people long to realize that deep in the heart of every man is the innate desire to learn. But many people have never thought about their responsibility to help others meet this basic need.

Not long ago while walking down the corridor of our headquarters I met one of the new secretaries.

"Hello, Miss Smith. Are you enjoying your work?"

"Oh, it's just wonderful. I've never been so happy in my life."

"Fine. I'm glad you like it."

"There's only one thing . . ."

"Yes?"

"Sometimes I think I should be paying them instead of their paying me."

"Why is that?"

"Well, it's just that I am learning so many important things I never knew before. Dr. Johnson, who gives me dictation, always explains the work, and by the end of the day I feel like I've been going to college and getting paid for it too!"

Later that day I began to think about what she had said. What a contrast between Dr. Johnson and most of us. By taking a little time to explain things to his secretary, he was helping to meet a basic psychological need in her life—the desire to learn and to understand.

Actually, we *all* have the responsibility (and privilege) to open lines of communication and to create an atmosphere in which those with whom we live and work can learn and gain knowledge. And in doing so, we also help ourselves.

In a sense, we are *all* teachers. What a challenge! It's up to us to help children and young people to learn. Whether they are in our family, our community, or in some other sphere of our influence, our responsibility remains.

We should never tell a child that he is too young or too stupid to understand. And when he raises the questions that are embarrassing or difficult for us to answer at the time, we should accept the child and his question, and let him know that we will think it over. It is no disgrace to admit that we do not have all the answers.

Much more important than the answer we give is the cordial, encouraging way in which we react to those who are inquiring. So many people grow to adulthood feeling that no one has time for them, that others are not interested in their questions. Such feelings can increasc to a point where serious maladjustments develop; and the results are physical and emotional disturbances.

Often I have found that teenagers and adults who had serious behavior problems or who, for example, have committed sex crimes, are really the victims of ignorance. They have done these things because they never had the opportunity to gain wholesome, factual information. This is to the shame of parents, schools and churches. Yes, we *do* have definite responsibilities to others—and in this way we also serve society.

Husbands and wives encourage each other to keep growing intellectually. Since gaining knowledge is one of the basic needs of man, meeting this need will help each marriage partner to be a happier, healthier person. Reading, taking courses, attending lectures, traveling, experimenting—these and many other activities will help keep your marriage zestful and romantic. They will add sparkle and interest to your home. And your children will admire you for it.

Information Plus

The most important dimension of knowledge is the "kind." To be sure, there is learning that yields great satisfaction. But much of our learning merely demands more learning. The man who plumbs the depths of learning doesn't always come up with a satisfied heart. How well we know that some of the most unhappy people in the world are those who have walked down graduation aisles to pick up impressive pieces of the "alphabet" by "degrees."

A few years ago I had the privilege of taking graduate study at Columbia University in New York City. During that time I became well acquainted with scholars from many parts of the world. If secular learning itself could make people happy, I was in the right place to see it. Nearly everyone I met was reaching a pinnacle of accomplishment—the doctor's degree! But I noticed little relationship between secular intellectual achievement and genuine peace and happiness. Something was lacking.

One fellow, John was typical. He often talked about how happy he would be when he completed his dissertation. When at last the University handed him the coveted sheepskin, I asked, "Well, John, how does it feel?" His answer did not surprise me. "I'm glad it's over," he said, "but it doesn't make me feel any different."

John's learning (volumes of it) had added up to innumerable facts and figures but not to immeasurable joy and gladness. Why? Because it revolved around the creature, not the creator. Its center was materialistic. God was forgotten. And the deep longings of the mind and heart still went begging.

The twentieth century is characterized by great advances in knowledge—unprecedented communication, sources of power, space travel, and many fantastic discoveries.

We pride ourselves in having made great strides. But for all this, it has not lessened the corruption of our society. The more we learn, the more clever we are at killing each other.

General Omar Bradley, the distinguished military leader, made this classical statement: "Our knowledge of science has clearly outstripped our capacity to control it. We have too many men of science; too few men of the Sermon on the Mount. The world has achieved brilliance without wisdom, power without conscience. Ours is a world of nuclear giants and ethical infants. We know more about war than we do about peace, more about killing than we do about living. This is our twentieth century's claim to distinction and progress."

In a recent book Charles A. Lindbergh wrote, "To me in youth, science was more important than either man or God. I worshipped science. Now I understand that spiritual truth is more essential to a nation . . . The more urgent mission of our time is to understand these (spiritual) truths and to apply them to our way of modern life."

When six Nobel prize winners, all top men of science representing five different nations, met in New York a few years ago, they gave this statement to the press: "Science has nothing to give men to change their nature so that they will stop fighting wars."

But the greatest statements about human learning and knowledge have been made by God Himself in the Bible. Describing people who live in the "last days," he says they are, "ever learning, and never able to come to the knowledge of the truth" (II Tim. 3:7).

Man-made satellites, guided missiles, space stations, and round trips to the moon! These are wonderful. But they do not bring satisfaction. And the heart of man still cries out, "Unsatisfied!"

Knowledge with Satisfaction

Is there any knowledge that can satisfy the human heart? May our desire to learn, to gain understanding be gratified?

Yes, there is Truth that sets you free, "knowing" that brings peace and happiness, knowledge that never disappoints the learner. This truth challenges all ranges of intelligence . . .

One evening several years ago I was glancing through the daily newspaper when suddenly a familiar name caught my eye. Immediately I followed the column with keen interest. We knew this man:

"Listen to this, honey," I said to my wife. And then I read the article about our friend.

How thrilled we were! This man was an educator, a man of degrees—but best of all, he was a born-again believer. As we read the news item it stated that he had taken the qualifying examination for the doctor's degree in a certain great university. Then it went on to say that he had come out with the *highest* I.Q. score ever recorded in that institution.

Several days later I saw this brilliant man. As we fellowshiped together and talked of the things of God, he said in all sincerity and humility, "Narramore, I am constantly amazed at the inexhaustibility of the Bible. I may study one chapter thoroughly, but the very next day I can study the same chapter again, and it will still unfold something that I had never seen before.

"Sometimes I wonder how I could have missed these marvelous things. But that's the way the Word of God is. I can study the same portion of Scripture day after day and month after month—and through the years there is always something more wonderful that I had not discovered before."

Yes, the Bible challenges man's highest intellect. And it is not until he follows Christ that he faces the greatest challenge. It is then that new vistas of knowledge open before him and he finds access to unlimited Truth.

What is this *knowledge*? What is the *Truth*?

Interestingly enough, Truth is a *Person!* Not facts? Not information? No, a Person. Jesus spoke with Divine authority when He said, "I am the Truth." (John 14:6). And in Colossians 2:3, the Bible tells us that in God and Christ "are hid all the treasures of wisdom and knowledge."

All the treasures of wisdom and knowledge—in God! That means, then, that if we are to have true wisdom, the kind that satisfies, we must go to the source, to God Himself. The Bible says: "The fear of the Lord is the beginning of wisdom." (Ps. 111:10).

Notice that we do not even *begin* to have wisdom until we reverently recognize God. Knowledge without God is built upon a wrong premise. Therefore, it is faulty. When God is left out, there is a God-sized vacuum in the center of man's knowledge. And all other knowledge is out of balance because the hub is missing.

In order to understand the "why of life" we must *first* realize our condition as sinners, unfit to stand in the presence of a Holy God. Then as we learn the truth of the Gospel—how God sent His only Son, Jesus, to die on the Cross for our sins—it is our responsibility to act upon this knowledge and accept Christ as our Saviour. When we have done this, we can experience the joy and peace of knowing that we belong to God—

that we are truly His redeemed children. Only when we know the Giver of life can we understand life. It then takes on meaning and purpose. "And we *know* that all things work together for good to them that love God, to them who are the called according to His purpose" (Rom. 8:28).

After we have been saved, we have an even greater incentive to learn. We want to be our best for God. Furthermore, learning is easy because our thinking is straight. It is God's command to "Study to shew thyself approved unto God, a workman that needeth not to be ashamed, rightly dividing the word of truth" (II Tim. 2:15).

As we grow in spiritual wisdom and understanding, guided by the Holy Spirit, we can say with the psalmist, "I have more understanding than all my teachers, for Thy testimonies are my meditation" (Ps. 119:99).

More than *teachers?* Yes, that is exactly what this verse says. It sounds strange, yet it is true. Your teachers may be loaded with systematized facts; they may be walking encyclopedias. Yet, if they do not know Christ, the fountainhead of all knowledge, they are sadly lacking in truth and in wisdom!

Man's knowledge does not last long. It is temporary at its best. Man may learn "facts" today but find them changing tomorrow. He goes from one bit of knowledge to another—groping, struggling and striving to find his way through the dark maze.

Yesterday's great knowledge is no longer great today. The newspaper is thrown away the day after it is printed. Encyclopedias are sold for a "song" after they are a few years old. One great invention passes into oblivion after another great discovery is made. So it is that information today is not what it was yesterday—or what it will be tomorrow.

But God's knowledge is not so. It lasts forever and ever. Man constantly strives to gain insight into even the "ABC's" of God's great wonders. Take the atom for example. Have you ever realized that the root words for "atom" means, "impossible to be split?" But the most interesting part is not that we have split the atom. It could have been done centuries ago. The significant fact is that man has split what he said was absolutely "unsplittable"! And so the word "atom" stands as a monument to man's unreliable, transient knowledge.

How God must smile as He looks down and sees us gloat in our own "great findings." God knew all the answers from the beginning, because "All things were made by Him; and without Him was not anything made that was made" (John 1:4). He knows the unknown!

But the believer is never left to the mercy of man's vacillating, changing theories. The Christian can say, "I will bless the Lord, who hath given me counsel: my reins [inner self] also instruct me in the night seasons." Regardless of world conditions, we can be sure that God's wisdom and knowledge shall be the stability of our times. God promises, "I will instruct thee and teach thee in the way which thou shalt go. I will guide thee with mine eye." And when God is "instructing" us we can know that we are on the right track.

Our library shelves are lined with encyclopedias and other books dealing with almost every conceivable subject—volume after volume. Yet, as complete as these may seem to be, they are still pitifully inadequate. They tell us only a smattering of truth—simply because they are the outgrowth of our limited, finite minds.

But there is one Book that stands apart from all others. This continual best-seller astounds the greatest scholars: it withstands the test of time. It is not of human origin; it is divinely inspired *without errors.* Down through the years it has been miraculously preserved. God's Book of knowledge, the Holy Bible, is as sure as God Himself because it is His Word. "Heaven and earth shall pass away but my Word shall not pass away" (Matt. 24:35).

The poet (author unknown) who penned the following lines pays sincere tribute to the BOOK OF BOOKS.

There are books in the making and books in the store,
There are books on the table, and books on the floor.
The library and stockroom have books piled up high,
There are more to be written and more I must buy.

Historical novels, biographies too;
Each week brings a dozen exhausting "Who's Who,"
There is fiction that's truthful, and fiction that's trash,
There's an orderly volume and another mere hash.

There's a new book of science and a book of the play,
There's the book of the year, and the book of the day.
There are books to refer to and some to ignore,
There are books that will thrill you and others will bore.

But the Book of the ages, of balance and power
Is the Book called the Bible, the Book of the hour!
Exhaustless its treasure, eternal its store
All the best of the others you'll find here—and more!

It is true that to be healthy and happy we should keep on learning. This desire to gain knowledge is a basic psychological need that cries out to be satisfied. But knowledge and education given solely from the minds of men are not adequate. We can search the libraries of the nations, gain all of the world's understanding and yet never find fulfillment in the empty shell of knowledge.

Not until a man accepts the Christ of the Bible as His own Saviour and lives a dynamic Christian life is this need completely satisfied. It is only then that the veil of understanding is lifted: his learning is no longer centered in his own finite little world, but in eternity. Now he can look "beyond"; now he has access to divine knowledge because God, his Father, is the very Author of knowledge!

6

How to Handle Fear

While working in my office one day, I received an urgent phone call. "Dr. Narramore," a young lady said, "my name is Jane White. I'm a Christian and I've read your articles in magazines. I need help—badly. May I speak to you for a minute?"

"Surely, are you free to talk from where you are now?"

"Yes," she gasped. "I'm in a phone booth. I just got off the bus. And please forgive me if I sound like—well, if I don't seem to make sense. But for weeks I've been having terrible fears. And just now while I was riding to work, that dreadful, frightening feeling began to come again. I tell you, I almost became hysterical. I didn't know who to call or what to do. But I knew of you so I got off the bus and phoned. I'm afraid I'll do something terrible if I don't get help. May I see you right away?"

I arranged an appointment. And as I put down the receiver, my heart went out to her in pity. True, I had worked with similar cases. But I was reminded again that there are *many* who suffer from fear, although their cases may not be as serious as Jane's.

Unrelieved fear is damaging to the mind and body. And it causes real *pain* and suffering.

God says, "Fear hath torment." It is a devastating thing. We may feel sorry for those who are fearful, but we cannot fully realize the torture that fear inflicts unless we have experienced it ourselves. True, fear knocks at everyone's door—no one is exempt. But unless we are fearful much of the time, we cannot know the mental anguish it brings and the toll it takes on the human body.

What Does Fear Do?

In his publication, "Your Emotions and God's Word," Harvey C. Roys, prominent medical doctor, illustrates the effect of fear. He tells of a laboratory experiment in which an animal was purposely frightened. Here are Dr. Roys' findings: "If you take a cat into the x-ray room and give it a special meal of Barium Sulphate, you can study by means of a fluoroscope the action of the cat's stomach. You will see that there are nice muscle waves which mix the food and cause the digestive processes to be carried on. Then if you bring a *dog* into the room, something happens. All of those beautiful muscle waves stop. The digestive processes cease, and the cat has indigestion. If this experiment is repeated enough times, the cat may develop a peptic ulcer."*

If this can happen to a cat—a mere animal, what then takes place when a complex, sensitive human being is subjected to fear? The answer is real suffering—physical as well as mental.

Fear takes on many physical symptoms. For years we have recognized such signs as upset stomach, headaches and nervousness. But today, the list is growing longer. Medical books are filled with ailments that stem from emotional disturbances such as fear.

Fear silently robs people of good health and happiness. They sense that something is wrong but they do not know the cause. So when this basic psychological need, *being relatively free from fear,* remains unmet in your life, you are certain to suffer the consequences—torment, mental anguish and physical damage.

**Your Emotions and God's Word,* Harvey C. Roys, M.D. (Seattle Gospel Publishing Service, Seattle, Washington). Quoted by permission of the author.

And the results of such emotional conflicts finally pile up, showing themselves in a variety of ways.

Have you ever wondered whether fears and anxieties can actually turn a person's hair white? It can! Researchers have found that severe emotional stresses can cause a rapid formation of microscopic air bubbles in the hair. These displace the natural pigment and cause the hair to appear white. This only emphasizes the profound and far-reaching effects of fear and worry.

In many cases, low scores on vision tests have been traced to anxiety. We find that in fifty out of every one hundred people, the ability to see is definitely impaired when they are even slightly frightened.

Fear can actually "scare the wits out of you," causing the thought processes to come practically to a halt. Even mild anxiety can hamper your ability to think. Unless you are forced to do so, it is foolish to tackle a tough problem or to make an important decision when you are anxious or fearful.

When a person is afraid, he cannot think as clearly or as rationally as he is ordinarily capable of doing. This is why fear interferes with learning.

Teachers who use fear to discipline students defeat their own purpose because it sets up mental blocks and hinders the learning process. Fear makes students "clam up," forgetting the things they already know: it also discourages creative thinking and reasoning. Actually, fear is a form of "mild panic"—you temporarily lose control of yourself. Such a condition never encourages learning.

How well I remember "Miss Larson," one of my high school teachers. I can see her yet—straight and austere with steel gray hair and cold gray eyes. She was there for business. She would tolerate no foolishness—and everyone knew it. When Miss Larson entered the room a peculiar spell came over the entire class. Cold chills ran up and down our spines. One thought flooded our minds, "I hope she doesn't call on me." But the inevitable was bound to come. And when it did, fear gripped not only our minds but also our vocal cords.

"Robert," she would command, "stand and report."

Like the others before him, Robert stood up in a daze of fear—his mind a complete blank. He had prepared his lesson and he knew it well. But under the circumstances, he simply could not remember.

It's a wonder he learned *anything* in that class. But I'm sure of this: the little we absorbed was *in spite* of her and not *because* of her teaching. Oh yes, she knew her subject and she was capable of teaching it, but the *fear* she instilled *prevented* us from learning.

How Fear Begins

Where does fear come from and how does it begin? Is it from training? Or through experience?

The answer is *both*. We learn fear from both training and experience. And it is important that we do.

Training? Yes. And a reasonable amount of caution is desirable. Children must learn to avoid hazardous traffic, fires, hot stoves, high places, and many other situations involving danger.

There is a limit, of course. Some parents go beyond this reasonable limit, instilling needless fear into their children, warning them of situations which are *not* actually harmful. Overcautious and oversolicitous adults sometimes protect children from imaginary dangers.

We as parents and teachers may have fears, and whether we realize it or not, by our actions and reactions we can impose these same fears upon our children. Fear is contagious. Children are especially susceptible when fear is imparted to them by their parents.

Take Phyllis, for example. She was afraid of many things—things her mother had feared. Oh yes, Phyllis was a grown woman, now married and with a family of her own. Although she realized that many of her fears were ungrounded, she couldn't seem to break her pattern of reactions.

Phyllis was horrified of spiders. If one should even come near her, she would become almost hysterical. Why? Because her mother had reacted that way.

And electrical storms—how they terrified her!

One day in my office, Phyllis began to talk about her fears. "I remember," she said, "how it was when we were children. Whenever there was a bad storm with thunder and lightning, mother would grab my sister and me and take us to a closet. There, all three of us would huddle, hide our faces and tremble until the storm had passed. You see, mother's uncle had been struck and killed by lightning. That was probably the reason for her intense fear.

"But as for my sister and me—well, I suppose mother 'taught' us to dread lightning and thunder. And although I realize now how foolish it is to become so panicky over an electrical storm, that terrible fear still grips me."

As Phyllis and I continued to talk about her fears, I admired the mature attitude she was taking in regard to her own small children.

"I'm determined not to make *my* children suffer from fear just because I do," she told me. "And no matter how frightened I am, I try to act as though it doesn't bother me at all."

"And are you successful?" I asked.

"Oh, yes," answered Phyllis. Then, as her face lit up in a radiant smile, she added, "And what's more, when I tell my children that these so-called fears are nothing to be afraid of, I not only help them, but I help *myself.*"

And Phyllis was right! She was not only helping her children to develop healthy, normal attitudes, but in so doing, she was helping herself.

But what about *experience*? Don't people develop fears because they have been frightened themselves?

Yes, and sometimes this is good. We *should* fear real danger. But it doesn't always end there. It may cause serious difficulty later on. Severe fright—either from a real cause or an imaginary one—if not relieved, understood, or realistically resolved, may be forgotten after a short time with no apparent reactions. But it is not at all uncommon for this fear (or a related one) to rear its ugly head again months or even years later. The person may develop a phobia that persists in spite of its irrationality—and the basic cause is none other than the frightful experience that left its hidden scar sometime before.

Bob, a young business man, was the victim of a hidden, unresolved fear. Symptoms: (1) although he had talent and training, he had a dread of speaking in public, and (2) he had a distressing dream that visited and revisited him. It was always the same—he couldn't remember his lines in a play.

Bob, like many people, had never told anyone about his fear. But it was a constant annoyance that kept him from being his best.

One evening while he was thumbing through a magazine, an article caught his eye. It was entitled, HIDDEN FEARS. He eagerly read every word. That did it!

I know what I'll do, thought Bob as he put down the magazine. *I'll go see a psychiatrist. Maybe I can get help like the fellow in this story.*

It was all set—every Tuesday at 4:00 o'clock. But Bob got cold feet and just before the first appointment, he almost backed out. However, once he broke the ice, he looked forward to the other interviews.

"Bob," said the psychiatrist at the end of several sessions, "what do you think? Do we need to get together any more?"

"No," Bob replied. "I think my problem is worked

out now. In fact, I'm *sure* it is settled. And thanks so much for all your help."

What had happened? During their sessions together, Bob had talked to the psychiatrist about his fears. The psychiatrist had encouraged him to discuss them in detail. Simply emptying his heart and mind gave Bob a great deal of relief. But the psychiatrist did not stop there. He skillfully arranged and guided the discussion so that Bob could explore in detail the possible causes of his fears. Bob examined each cause carefully and looked for a connection between it and his present condition. Little by little he uncovered the roots to his problem. He traced back into his own experiences until he found the beginnings of his fears. Then he brought them out into the open, examined them, talked about them until each one was finally whittled down to its true, insignificant size. Now that the causes were understood, resolved and "aired," Bob cleaned out both large and small particles of fear residue that had quietly and secretly haunted him for years.

What causes fear? Unfortunately, as in Bob's case, the causes are not always obvious. In fact, they may be extremely subtle and difficult to uncover. Since fear is an emotion, it is often tied up with other emotional problems. Studies reveal that people who are from broken homes, or who have personality problems, are much more likely to have ungrounded fears. But in extreme cases, a person needs individual study and diagnosis before intelligent treatment or therapy can take hold.

Fear does not always develop suddenly. And although it may *seem* to have just arisen, more often it is the result of a series of experiences which accumulate until they seem like mountains.

Take Marjorie, for example—a nice looking girl with a sincere, pleasant personality. People liked Marjorie because she liked them. Her difficulty did not show up until she was married.

Her mother had always "taken care of things" and was recognized for her efficiency. But after Marjorie began housekeeping for herself, she found she had a problem. She was afraid to entertain guests. Oh yes, she wanted to be sociable. She and her husband Dick were popular with their age group at church. But Marjorie had no confidence in her ability to cook or graciously serve guests in her home. Sound foolish? Yes, to some, but not to Marge.

The reason for Marjorie's fear: from the time she was a little girl, her mother had never allowed her to help in the kitchen. "Now run along, dear," mother would protest when Marjorie wanted to help. "I don't want to be bothered when I'm cooking. I can do this much better and faster than you can—so run along and do something else."

That was not all. Marjorie's older sister was a "natural" at cooking. "My, how well Roberta does," people would remark. "She just seems to have a knack."

But not Marjorie! She just *didn't* have the "knack" —*nor was it ever developed.* When she tried her hand at cooking, it usually ended in failure. But worse than that, the family laughed at her. The result: Marjorie was *afraid to try.*

Yes, our childhood fears often carry over into adulthood, causing maladjustments in later life. If a person has never developed self assurance as a child, he cannot suddenly expect to have it when he is grown. And so it was with Marjorie.

But Marjorie's story *does* have a happy ending. Dick proved to be an understanding husband who was able to help Marjorie gain the self-confidence that had been denied her for so many years. He encouraged her to talk about her problem. He tried never to ridicule her, either privately or in public. And Dick's approval of her efforts became a real "boost" to Marjorie. He was always on hand to compliment her (even if her cooking wasn't like "Mother's"). Not only that, he encouraged her to take a course in home management. This gave her the "know-how" she lacked. With this kind of encouragement from her partner, it wasn't long before Marjorie's self-confidence began to blossom. And her fear? Well, that slowly disappeared.

Yes, as in Marjorie's case, we can help each other. We have a responsibility to our children—and to our marriage partner. Since people are not perfect, it is possible that an excellent marriage may have one partner who lacks self-confidence and is beset by fear. But if the other one is patient and understanding and works intelligently, a great deal can be done to alleviate these fears. How much better to help a person than to blame! Fear is always caused: but if we do our part, we can help others overcome their fears and be more like the people God intended them to be.

Nipped in the Bud

A wise man once said, "The best remedy for fear is to meet it before it happens." How true this is. When you fear something, don't run away—analyze it. Then you can decide the course of action to take. Truly, inaction is fear's greatest ally, and action is the most effective antidote.

Since "an ounce of prevention is worth a pound of cure," Christian parents and teachers can do much to prevent boys and girls from developing phobias. How? By candidly examining their methods of control, making sure that they rarely use *fear* as a means of discipline. The "fear method" is not only unsound; it is *unkind.*

"Do it or I'll tell the bogey man to get you!" "If you don't behave, I'll give you away to someone else!" "If you say that word again they'll cut your tongue off!" "If you don't do it, I'll lock you in that dark closet!" "If you don't act nicer, I won't love you any more!"

We have all heard people use ultimatums of this kind—and perhaps we've been guilty of resorting to similar ones ourselves. True, fear-laden threats such as these may bring immediate results. But they can inflict emotional damage that will leave a permanent scar.

How much better it is to honestly spank a child or take away his privileges than to dangle the weapon of fear over his head—a force with which he cannot cope.

Naturally, we should teach chidren to respect common dangers. But we should do all in our power to prevent them from being unduly fearful. When a child is fearful of a definite object or situation, we can help by entering the situation with him, minimizing the danger, and little by little showing him that there is nothing to fear.

Understanding Minimizes Fear

Have you ever realized that we seldom fear the things we understand? That is why it is so important for parents to talk with children about their fears. Understanding may not cause us to like certain things, but it does keep us from fearing them.

A young lady named Beth once told me her experience.

"When I was a little girl we lived on a street lined with huge trees," Beth said. "I don't remember what kind of trees these were, but I *do* know that in the spring of the year they dropped strange reddish blossoms—about as big around as a pencil and approximately two or three inches long. When people walked down the street and stepped on them, these blossoms would squash on the sidewalk and make what to me looked like a disgusting mess.

"I was deathly afraid of these blossoms," Beth continued, "because I did not realize what they really were. I thought they were ugly worms. And I had no special love for worms.

"I hated to go outside as long as those 'worms' were there. And when I walked to and from school I can remember hopping from one clear spot to another in order to avoid stepping on those repulsive 'creatures.' They almost made me sick.

"Then one day my kind, understanding mother found out about this strange fear that haunted me. She did not ridicule, but lovingly took me aside and explained that these were *not* worms at all but blossoms that preceded the leaves. 'Soon,' she told me, 'they will come out in all their glory to dress the barren trees in a lovely green robe.' Then picking up one of these blossoms, she held it gently in her hand. 'See, it is not a worm at all,' she said sweetly. 'It is a flower. See how pretty it is!'

"And for the first time in several springtimes, I saw beauty, not ugliness, in these fallen blossoms. Yes, they *were* rather pretty when I looked at them closely.

"I still did not *like* these blossoms, but now I was no longer afraid. I saw them in a different light. And, in time, I did not mind them at all."

Preparation Reduces Fear

People are fearful of the unknown. And the unknown does not necessarily mean any more than the untried. Actually, it makes little difference whether the untried is a person's first airplane ride or a child's first day at school.

Adults should prepare children for new experiences—getting them ready to accept rather than fear them. It is an important aspect of good social development.

I cannot help but think of Jimmie. His reaction to a new experience was a common one.

It was a beautiful clear day in early September. But as Jimmie walked beside his mother up the broad stone steps of the Westwood Elementary School, a strange apprehension gripped him. Jimmie reached up, grasped his mother's hand, and squeezed it tightly. He shuddered.

"What's the matter, Jimmie?" asked Mother.

"I'm cold. I don't feel well. I want to go home."

"Are you sick?" Mother looked at Jimmie half anxiously—half inquiringly—and a little bit dubiously.

"Yes," he blurted out, "I'm sick. I don't want to go to school."

"Oh, so that's it! But darling, you *have* to go to school."

"No, I don't want to."

"But why?"

"Because—because I'm—I'm afraid!"

Jimmie wasn't putting on. He really *was* afraid. Afraid because he was facing a new situation—afraid because he did not know what to expect.

When Jimmie stepped into the classroom and saw all the strange faces, he did not feel any better. He stuck close to his mother, still insisting that he did not want to stay.

"But you *have* to stay, Jimmie," persisted his mother.

"Then you stay *with* me. Don't leave me, Mommie. Don't leave me." Jimmie's pleading was earnest as he clung to his mother.

By this time Mother was becoming disgusted with her young son—but in an effort to calm him she promised that she would not leave.

Jimmie was satisfied. With Mother near, he felt safe.

But she had no intention of staying. So as soon as the teacher had Jimmie's eye, Mother slipped away.

The next morning Jimmie and his mother started out for school again. But the situation had not improved. Jimmie was more insistent than ever: *he did not want to go*. And today, *two* fears confronted him—the fear of a new situation (the classroom) and the fear that his mother would not keep her word.

Many children are afraid of new experiences. But the problem is never solved by deceit. Parents should *talk* with children and *explain* in a quiet, positive manner just what to expect. Then be sweetly firm—but *always* honest.

THE WRONG METHODS

Ridicule and teasing do not help a person who is afraid. It offers no solution—only adds embarrassment to the present fear. And the fear of being embarrassed is a most uncomfortable one. It is psychologically unsound to try to embarrass people out of their fears. It does no good—only harm—to drag a person's fears out in front of his friends. It makes him feel that he "loses face" with them. And fears are never overcome by tearing down confidence.

Some people think that they can help a frightened person by "forcing" him. Or perhaps they may take the unsuspecting victim by surprise to try to prove to him that he need not be afraid. But this is wrong. No doubt the people who do these things are well meaning—but they are not aware of the consequences. Because fear is not resolved by shock—rather, it is intensified. And this kind of "help" only makes matters worse.

I will never forget Diane's case. She did not like feathers. In fact, the repulsion was so intense that she actually feared them. No, she could not be coaxed to touch even the tiniest feather.

This seemed silly—especially to her brothers, Phil and Dan. "Imagine," they said, "being afraid of a little, soft, harmless feather."

At first Diane's brothers laughed and teased about it, but when their sister continued to be afraid, they became impatient. "We must do something to make her get over this crazy notion," they said.

Oh, they meant no harm—but it was not only *what* they did but *how* they did it. And the damage they inflicted was permanent.

It was Saturday noon. Diane had been playing with some neighbor children. Phil and Dan waited until Mother called her in for lunch. Then they hid behind a bush near the front door. The trap was set, and Diane was the unsuspecting victim.

A minute later, Diane, bubbling over with joy, arrived at the front door.

And then it happened!

Phil, standing behind the door, held a feather pillow that he and Dan had opened on one end. And as Diane entered the house, they showered her with feathers, shaking the entire pillow over her head!

What a joke! The boys roared—for a minute.

But it wasn't a joke to Diane. It was a horrible, frightening nightmare. Phil and Dan grew serious when they saw their sister's terrified expression and heard her hysterical screams. What had they done?

Diane was beside herself. She lost all control as this awful, traumatic experience seized her. Nothing the boys or their parents could do would calm or quiet her. Diane became weak—nauseated—a severe chill shook her entire body. She was a sick girl.

When the doctor arrived, his diagnosis was "a severe case of shock." It was several days before Diane was well enough even to sit up in bed.

But physical damage was not the only result. The extreme emotional upheaval that took place within Diane was of far more lasting consequence.

She is a grown woman today. But she still breaks out in a cold sweat whenever she sees a feather. And as a result of this ill-timed experience, she developed several other fears that she has never been able to conquer. Confidence in her brothers and in her whole world was shattered that fateful day—it lay at her feet in a shamble of tiny, white feathers—confidence that was never restored. Nor did the horror of this experience ever cease to linger in her mind. The result? It added to her insecurity. And today, she is a restricted fearful personality—because someone tried to "force" her out of her fear.

Another foolish way to handle fears is to simply say, "Relax!" Merely telling a person to relax is no solution. If he *could* relax, he would. Admonitions to relax neither change the facts nor one's attitudes. They merely leave a frightened person where he was—frightened without a sympathetic friend. But talking it out *does* help.

So let him do the talking. Encourage him to tell you how he feels. It's much more effective. After all, what *you* think doesn't automatically change *his* feelings. Fear is a gripping thing—you can't get away from it. And no matter how foolish it may seem to others, it is real to the one who is caught in its clutches.

How can we help people overcome their fears? Certainly not by ignoring them. Just saying, "You shouldn't be afraid," is pure folly. People must be reassured, comforted and put in a more secure situation. Then they will be able to see things in a clearer perspective. Then the feared circumstance will not seem so foreboding.

Take the case of little Timmy. He was afraid of the dark.

Every night it was the same. Daytime was a happy time, but when darkness came, something happened inside of Timmy.

When it was time to go to bed, he would stall as long as he could—a story, a drink of water—and, of course, the bathroom! And so it went, until his exasperated mother would finally corral him into his bed, give him a final goodnight kiss, and tuck the covers snugly around his little shoulders.

Then came the dreaded moment when mother reached to turn out the light.

"Oh, Mommie, please don't! Please don't turn off the light!"

"But Timmy," rebuked his mother, "it's time to go to sleep." She reached again toward the lamp.

"No, Mommie. Please!" There was real urgency in Timmy's pleading voice. His eyes portrayed a look of terror as he gasped, "I'm—I'm afraid! It's so dark when the light is out."

"Afraid? Afraid of the *dark?* Why Timmy," she chided, "a big boy like you *afraid* of the dark. How silly! What would your friends think of you if they knew? I'm ashamed of you."

And with that she reached determinedly for the light, clicked it off, and strode out of his room, closing the door behind her.

Timmy buried his head under the covers and shuddered. Deep, insistent sobs shook his little body. His throat felt strangely dry. He was afraid. He didn't want to be—but he was. And he was suffering *needlessly*—and alone.

Little wonder that Timmy hated bedtime. And little wonder, too, that he developed many other fears which followed him all through his life and kept him from being the well adjusted man he should have been.

How much wiser Timmy's mother would have been had she taken a cue from Susan's mother.

Susan was afraid too. But when her mother found out what was troubling her, she bought a little night light and put it in Susan's room. And sometimes, when Susan seemed especially fearful, her mother sat by her bed and talked with her reassuringly.

"Everything is all right, honey," she would tell her. "Mother and Daddy are here in the next room and we'll leave the door open. Then if you need us, you can call us. But even better than that, Jesus is right here with you all of the time. You know that He loves you. We all love you, darling, and we're going to take care of you."

It wasn't long until Susan forgot that she had ever been afraid—and all through her life she learned to combat fear with confidence.

God and Fears

Yes, there are many reasonable, effective ways to minimize fear, both in our own lives and in the lives of others. And God expects us to use the intelligence that He has given us.

But human techniques are not enough. At best, our wisdom and understanding are hampered by human limitations. Psychological needs met solely on this level are never met adequately. *It is God who completely understands our basic needs.* And He has made provision to meet them in ways far superior to man's.

Several years ago I received a telephone call that I shall always remember. As I picked up the receiver, a lady's voice said, "Dr. Narramore, I'm Mrs. Newton. I have some serious problems and I would like to make an appointment to see you."

I explained that my schedule was filled for some time ahead and I told her that I was sorry but I would be unable to see her.

Yet she persisted. She went on to say that she had heard me speak over the radio and felt that I was the only one who could *really* help her. She told me how she had gone to "nearly everyone in Hollywood and Los Angeles" but how she was "no better off" than when she started.

Since I receive many calls from Christians who need counsel, I took it for granted that she too was a believer. But in the course of our conversation, I remarked, "I suppose that you know the Lord."

"Who?"

"I suppose you know the Lord."

"No, Dr. Narramore, I don't believe that I do. I don't believe I've ever met him. Does he live around here?"

I was taken back. I knew then that God would have me arrange my schedule so that I could see her at least for a short time.

"Hold the phone," I told her, "I'll see what I can do to squeeze in an appointment for you." So I shaved off a little time here and there from several of my appointments and managed to scrape up half an hour that I could give her.

Three o'clock the next afternoon found Mrs. Newton seated in my office. She was a middle-aged lady, rather tall, well dressed and nice appearing. As we talked together, I found that she was a forthright, intelligent, reasonable person. After a few minutes I asked her to describe her difficulty.

"Well," she said, "I don't know what's wrong, but something is. Things aren't going right in my marriage. But that's not the only trouble. I am never satisfied and I don't have any peace. I seem to feel afraid inside, but I can't put my finger on any one particular thing. Oh, my fears aren't big—but just little ones that keep nagging at me all the time."

"What have you done about it?" I asked.

"Well," Mrs. Newton replied, "I made up my mind I had to do *something*. So I talked with a friend of mine who told me she thought my trouble was all personality centered, and that I ought to take a course in personality development. So I followed her suggestion and enrolled in a class where nearly fifty people met each week. We spent a lot of time talking about our problems, and we also wrote a short autobiography. A little later on we used much of our class time in public speaking. Most of us gave several short talks while the other members of the class evaluated our speeches in terms of self-confidence and personality development."

"How did you get along?" I asked.

"Very well," she said. "In fact, at the end of the first term the class voted me as having made the most progress in the group. Well, that was encouraging, so I decided to take the second term. This time I got along so well that the teacher asked me to be her assistant. When she wasn't there, I took over the class and taught it myself. And once again, when the term was over I was chosen as the one who had made the greatest improvement. In fact, they gave me a lovely pen and pencil set as a prize for having won this honor."

"Do you feel that you were really helped?" I asked her.

"Certainly not!" Mrs. Newton replied emphatically. Then shaking her head sadly, she continued, "If *I* was the one who had made the most improvement, I pity the others. Of course, I learned a little about speaking in public and I learned that other people have similar problems to mine. But I can't truthfully say that I felt any different after the courses than I did before I started."

"What did you do after that?"

"Well, at first I didn't know what to do. But after a while I got to thinking about the teacher of the class. We had become quite friendly during the course of the year and I thought that perhaps she could help me. So I went over to see her."

"And what happened?"

"Oh, not much! It was really kind of silly now that I look back on it. You see, when I told this lady about my fears and how I was afraid that I was losing my husband, she said she feared that she was losing hers too. She told me how she had let her first and second husbands slip right through her fingers. 'But,' she said, 'I'm not going to let that happen again. And since we are both afraid that we may lose our husbands, I'd suggest that we each set up an *ironclad* program to hold them.' "

Ironclad! I had to smile to myself. "That's strong," I said. "Did you do it?"

"No, Dr. Narramore. I realized that if she had such a serious problem herself, surely she wasn't in any condition to help *me*. She needed help more than I did."

"What did you do then?"

"To be very frank," she continued, "I didn't know what to do. I thought I had tried everything. Then yesterday I heard you speak over the radio and I decided that it might help if I could talk with you."

As we delved into her problem, I found that her childhood had been quite normal. Although her marriage had a few ups and downs, it was evidently fairly successful. Her financial condition was average. But the most important aspect of her life, the *spiritual*, was essentially blank. Except for a little Sunday school and church attendance now and then, nothing had ever happened.

Here, then, was my cue. I knew that this spiritual void in her life was the underlying cause of *all* her problems. So I started from the beginning and explained to her that God created man for Himself. People were never intended to go through life without the fellowship of their Maker. Without God, we have no purpose in life. We are like a ship sailing through a treacherous sea without a pilot. Destination—disaster! I explained how man, in his natural state, can have no communion or fellowship with God because God has a righteous, holy nature, and man has a sinful nature.

"But, Mrs. Newton," I added, "God loved us *so* much that He made a plan to bridge the gap, thus making it possible for us to get right with God."

Then I went on to tell her about God's plan—how He gave His only Son to atone for our sins and make peace for us. I told her that the Bible says, "Christ is our peace." In other words peace is not a state of mind. Peace is a Person. And that Person is Christ.

"Mrs. Newton," I asked, "have you ever invited Christ, the Prince of Peace, to come into your heart and life?"

She lowered her eyes for a moment, then said, "No, Dr. Narramore, I don't believe I ever have."

"Are you interested?"

"Oh yes," she answered. "It's all new to me, but I am *very* interested. In fact, I think this spiritual lack in my life may be the cause of my problem."

Then I asked her if she would like to accept Christ as her Saviour and invite Him to come into her heart and life.

"I surely would," she said. "I think this is just what I need."

So right then and there Mrs. Newton and I knelt in my office. "Dear God," she prayed. "I'm a sinner but I need You. Please come into my heart and save me. I promise that I'll serve You the rest of my life. For Jesus' sake. Amen."

When we stood up, her eyes glistened with moisture but her lips wore a smile. A look of peace swept across her face. I talked to her a minute more about what she had done in accepting Christ as her personal Saviour. Then I suggested that she read through the Gospel of John and memorize some verses—John 1:12; John 5:25 and John 10:28 were all excellent ones for a new Christian.

Mrs. Newton was a happy woman when she left that afternoon. She knew now that she was right with God and she was confident that He would guide her.

The following week I saw her once again. What a difference! She didn't even *look* the same. Now her countenance beamed with a radiance that reflected the peace and contentment of her soul.

As we talked she told me how she had already read several books of the Bible, had memorized a number of Scripture verses and had talked with God each day in prayer. No wonder she was growing—no wonder there was a change!

She looked up and smiled as she said, "Do you know, Dr. Narramore, I've had more *peace* this past week than I've had in my whole life!"

Her problems? Oh yes, she still had some. But now she had peace of heart and mind, knowing that God would help her over the rough places.

This fine lady found what she needed. True, her fears had not been too evident—but they were deep-seated in her nature and in her soul. She was not at rest, she had no peace—until Christ came into her heart. So it is with every human being. And not until we have been reconciled to God through His Son, Jesus Christ, can we ever know real peace and joy and the "perfect love that casteth out fear."

Life has its pleasant places—but it is far from a "bed of roses." As people reach adulthood they learn that life holds many tragedies. When confronted with illness, dread diseases, war, sudden failure, hunger, insecurity, severe injury, loneliness, old age and death, there is *cause* for fear. Our generation is rapidly distinguishing itself by the development of frightening new weapons of war. Earth satellites, guided missiles, interplanetary travel do not reassure the fearful heart of man.

But God, our Father, promises never to leave us nor forsake us. In our weakness He speaks to us, "Fear thou not; for I am with thee; be not dismayed; for I am thy God; I will strengthen thee . . ." (Isa. 41:10). And when tragedy comes God reassures us by saying, "When thou passest through the waters, I will be with thee; and through the rivers, they shall not overflow thee . . ." (Isa 43:2).

God does not promise escape from every fearful situation, but He does promise to walk with us through every experience! And we can be strong and unafraid because God is the strength of our life.

God tells us to "be *anxious* for *nothing*, but in everything by prayer and supplication with thanksgiving let your requests be made known unto God" (Phil. 4:6).

Here then, is a much better solution than being anxious. This solution is workable, while anxiety works nothing but havoc.

Just what does anxiety do? It does not empty tomorrow of its sorrow; but it does empty today of its strength. It does not make you escape the evil, it makes you unfit to cope with it when it comes. It does not bless tomorrow, but it robs today.

One basic fear common to all mankind is the fear of *death.* This is natural because deep inside the soul of every living creature is a strong desire to keep living. And indeed, death is grim, stark and unevasive. From childhood, every person knows that he is born to die. And when a person faces an unknown, uncertain eternity, he is a fool if he does not fear it.

I'll never forget the comment made by one of my professors at Columbia University. He was lecturing to a psychology class when he admitted that he was at a complete loss to know how to counsel about death.

"Students," he told us, "in all other cases of counseling I am confident, but in the face of death, there is *nothing* I can say."

Nothing? How hopeless! No wonder people are afraid!

But it doesn't need to be like this. Because Christ has *conquered* death, thereby taking away its sting and ugliness. And when we trust in Christ as our personal Saviour, eternity is a *bright and glorious prospect!* Death no longer is something to be feared—but rather something to be anticipated. Why? Because the child of God knows that to be absent from the body is "to be present with the Lord."

So for the Christian, death should hold no fear. And like the apostle Paul we too can say, "For me to live is Christ, but to die is gain" (Phil. 1:21). At death, the unsaved man has everything to lose. But the saved has everything to gain!

God has given us a wonderful promise—one that can dispel all fear. He says, "Lo, I am with you alway, even unto the end of the world" (Matt. 28:20).

This means, then, that circumstances cannot sever us from Him. It means that surroundings cannot hide God's face from us. He is always near and dear to those who are truly His own. Tests may come. He is near. Trials may come. He is still near. Sickness may lay us low. He is by our side. Death mav come, He still says, "Lo, I am with you alway." Nothing will be able to separate us from His love. Truly, we can say with the psalmist, "Yea, though I walk through the valley of the shadow of death, *I will fear no evil*: for thou art with me" (Ps. 23:4).

Peace of mind? Yes, it's part of the Christian's built-in blessing. Yet there are some Christians who do not appropriate this peace. True, they belong to God—but they do not *rely* on Him. They take affairs into their own hands and become upset and fearful. How unnecessary. How foolish. Happiness is at their command if they will only "cast their burden upon the Lord." Then, they too can say, "The Lord is my *light* and my *salvation;* whom shall I fear? The Lord is the *strength* of my life; of whom shall I be *afraid*?" (Ps. 27:1). What does God give us? Light. Salvation. But that is not all—He gives us strength and *no* fear!

Dr. Gilbert L. Little is a prominent physician with years of experience as a private psychiatrist and as head of a large American hospital. In his book, *Nervous Christians,** Dr. Little throws light on the subject of Christians who have fears. He emphasizes the following causes and solutions.

1. *Fear begins to enter a Christian's life the moment he starts losing close fellowship with God.*

Where does fear come from? Not from God. God is *love.* And "there is no fear in love" (I John 4:18). When we move away from God we leave the center of love and peace. God never creates disturbance in the heart of the consecrated believer. "For God is *not* the author of confusion, but of peace . . ." (I Cor. 14:33).

With God we have nothing to fear. He is our Father.

* Little, Gilbert L., *Nervous Christians* (1956, Good News Broadcasting Association, Inc.). Now published by Moody Press. Used by permission.

He cared for us in His infinite wisdom and love. What could be more reassuring? What could be more complete? Truly, when we "*abide* under the shadow of the Almighty" we have nothing to fear. So it is that the Christian who is in close harmony with God has no real cause for fear.

Is there fear in your heart? Then check your fellowship with God.

2. *When a believer begins to lose his close fellowship with God, he usually tries to cover up, seek his own devices, make excuses and use various compensation mechanisms.*

Adam did. And so did Eve. When they turned away from God, they attempted to cover up their guilt, fear and sin. And their descendants (you and I) are no different. We are still doing this today.

Adam and Eve did not turn back to God—the One they had offended. They did not beg forgiveness. Instead . . . "they sewed fig leaves together, and made themselves aprons" (Gen. 3:7). This was man's solution to hide his nakedness and sin. Christians are busy sewing "aprons" today—church "aprons" and many other kinds of "aprons."

We have no record that Adam feared while he loved God and communed with Him. He feared *after* he sinned. Spiritual Christians testify to this Scriptural truth today: as long as they love God and follow His will for their lives, they have no fear.

3. *When a Christian develops rather serious fears, he may tend to avoid counsel from a deeply spiritual person.*

When the Lord asked the disciples if they also would go away (to the world) Peter answered the question by saying, "Lord, to whom shall we go? Thou hast the words of eternal life" (John 6:68).

"To whom *shall* we go?"

Spiritual Christians should not expect non-Christians to help them with their problems of fear and anxiety, because non-Christians cannot understand soul problems. It is unfair to expect them to grasp spiritual things, which can be discerned only by the Spirit of God within the Christian.

It seems that most Christians, after suffering for many years, just assume that God has overlooked and forgotten the time when they turned to the world and forsook their "first love." Most of these people have really not repented of their backsliding, but have taken on religious or other works as a covering for sin. And when they do attempt to return to God, Satan discourages them by blocking their prayers and hindering the reading of the Word.

It is not unusual for Christians to decide quite suddenly, even during the period of psychotherapy, "I think I can go home and work out my problem by myself. I know what I should do." But sooner or later they go elsewhere for treatment.

Clients who have been "let down," in prior consultations tread warily the next time. Their complaint is, "I told him everything, but he didn't do a thing for me." These situations are unfortunate, but Christians should *not expect* the ungodly to help them resolve problems that have a spiritual cause. It is rebellion on the part of God's redeemed children, who are blood-bought, to turn from Him and go to the world with their spiritual problems.

The spiritual Christian trusts Christ to lead him much like a child trusts his father to lead him by the hand through difficult and fearful places. This does not take away the *object* of fear, or make him forget it. But now he is no longer afraid, because he trusts his father. And since God is our Heavenly Father, He leads us to overcome our fears.

4. *The way back to peace of mind is through confession, turning to Christ and walking daily with Him.*

Most people who are fearful would give anything to have their minds free from anxiety and worry. But this is not accomplished by treating symptoms. One must confess the things that made him anxious and guilty. Confession, however, must have a basis more substantial than a psychological release, which many people experience by merely confessing something. If there is to be a lasting therapeutic value in confession, man must come to the understanding that only confession from the heart and repentance toward God will bring healing to his soul and peace to his mind.

Confession does not imply a lengthy analysis of the subconscious memory. But the Christian does need to see how he was led to stray from God and how to find his way back to Calvary.

One of psychotherapy's big problems is to help a person see that his suffering developed over a long period of time, and that he cannot expect a few psychiatric consultations to do anything miraculous for him. He needs to go back . . . back; for it is usually a long way back to the place where he lost his "first love." The Lover of his soul has been pushed into the background and now he is preoccupied with himself.

The Christian who is afraid must turn his thoughts back to Calvary and get a fresh vision of Christ's redemptive love for him. *He must meditate, moment by moment*, on what Christ did and how He overcame for him.

In addition to Dr. Little's four basic considerations of fear, there are undoubtedly some fears that may be traced in part to physical origins. Remember the case of Jane White, the young lady who in desperation got off the bus and called me from the phone booth? Diagnosis indicated that her serious emotional and fearful state stemmed partially from a glandular malfunction. Medication not only gave her temporary relief, but it also undoubtedly helped to restore a proper chemical balance in the body. She also responded favorably to counseling from a Christian psychologist. Yes, Jane was a believer, but little did she realize how far she had strayed from God. The road back to Calvary was long and tedious. But through complete confession and submission she entered God's glorious joy and light.

True consecration to God, abundant prayer, and a continual feeding upon His Word provide the Christian with a way of life that dispels fear. It is then that "the peace of God, which passeth all understanding, shall *keep your hearts and minds* through Christ Jesus" (Phil. 4:7).

Surely, when we trust in Christ and lean hard on Him, we can say, "God hath not given us the spirit of fear; but of power, and of love and of a sound mind" (II Tim. 1:7).

7

Economic Security

ICE CRACKLED beneath the sleigh as the swift team of huskies pulled across the frozen terrain. Only the occasional bark of the dogs or the snap of the driver's whip interrupted the sound of the howling wind. Although it was only mid-afternoon, the sky was dark against the gleaming whiteness of the barren glaciers. This was Winter. And in Eskimo land the sun had gone to bed for the season.

Two fur-clad figures clung to the rear of the sleigh—Roy Atungurach, the driver, and his ten-year-old son, Tom. The sleigh was mostly filled with their cargo—a polar bear, two large seals and a barrel of fish.

A hunting expedition? Indeed! But these two Eskimos were not returning from an excursion that had been planned merely for pleasure and sportsmanship. They were struggling for the bare necessities of life—for food, shelter and clothing. And in their primitive culture, fishing and hunting supplied these needs.

True, Eskimos like Roy and Tom Atungurach do not spend a minute worrying about money for a new car or for dental bills or for health insurance or for education. But theirs is a day-to-day battle for food and clothing. Their quest for economic security is starkly real and brutally exhausting.

And while Eskimos are battling the economic problems of an unkind climate, the oil company executive in California is maneuvering just as fiercely against the economic forces he confronts. His college-age daughter demands a new sports car and Fifth avenue clothes to keep up with her sorority sisters. His insurance premiums are staggering. Taxes have soared. The upkeep on his $75,000 home is more than he bargained for. And in the shadowy background is the uneasy fear that he may lose his high-paying job, or if he does keep it, he will be unable to live on a retirement check of $750 a month.

Fortunately, these extremes don't affect the majority. Most of us are somewhere in between. But wherever we are—whatever our station or rank, *we all have a genuine need for at least a measure of economic security.* And this need is basic—not only to our physical well being, but also to our mental health. It is more than materialistic; it is psychological as well.

We *all* like to believe that some day we will be financially secure, that we will be able to retire comfortably in old age. We are hopeful that as the "rocking chair" days come, we will be able to pay our own way —not to be a burden on others. This is a natural desire of the human heart. And it's commendable.

But even a quick glance at our world tells us that people often go to *extremes.* This one insatiable drive seems to control their motives: "We must have financial security!"

The Scurry for Security

Every day millions of people feverishly expend their energies in activities which they hope will make them economically secure. With one eye on the bank account, they work days, nights, Sundays and overtime to bring in a few more dollars.

Some are overly concerned about the success of their business. They try nearly every trick of the trade to make their profits soar.

Housewives bravely fight the battle of the bargain. Anything to save a few pennies—even if they have to go out of their way to do it!

Others worry about stocks and bonds. Each day a

great network of communication advises people when to buy and when to sell. Blood pressures rise and fall with the temperamental fluctuations of Wall Street.

Insurance salesmen use countless "confidential" techniques to persuade the average man that he "cannot afford to be without adequate protection." After all, the salesman argues, "You owe it to yourself and to your family."

So it is in every realm of life. People work, strive and connive to assure themselves that they will be secure. True, we *do* need to provide for today and save for a "rainy day"—but most people seem to forget that God owns the cattle on a thousand hills. And so they eagerly stash away money and possessions without even giving God so much as a second thought.

After that it is only a matter of time: money looms up so big and important that it blots out real values and it practically becomes a god. This is the beginning of trouble. Because God warns that "the *love* of money is the root of all evil" (I Tim. 6:10).

Attitudes and Health

Man's inner drive to accumulate wealth usually goes far beyond the desire to meet his actual needs. It passes the point of "making a living." If possible, most people will settle for nothing less than protection against every emergency. And it is this ceaseless human search for financial security that often leads a man into difficulty. Hard work and constant struggle take their toll on the human body. But an even greater menace is hidden in the worry and concern involved. These affect both man's physical and mental condition.

Ralph Blake, for example, was such a victim. He was only in his thirties but he had complained of extremely poor health for some time. After a thorough physical examination, his doctor diagnosed the illness as one that was undoubtedly brought on by emotional tensions.

"Ralph," the doctor explained, "you need the services of a psychiatrist."

"What?" Blake exclaimed. "I may be sick, Doc, but I'm not crazy!"

"No, you're not crazy, and you probably never will be," assured the doctor. "But I think your worries and tensions have become so firmly fixed that you will need a specialist to help you find your way out. I doubt if you can get to feeling like you should until you resolve these feelings."

As Blake took trips to the psychiatrist's office the truth came to the top. The major causes of his nervous condition were the constant fears of not being able to support his family and not being able to handle financial emergencies should they arise.

Since the time he was a small boy, Blake's father had impressed on him the need for financial security. "Son," his father would admonish, "life is a very serious matter, and if you don't want to starve to death, you'd better work and save every cent you can." His parents often reminded him that people who were not able to pay their bills were taken to jail. They warned him against getting married early and having a family for whom he couldn't provide. In short, they filled his mind with so much concern that they were partially responsible for bringing about a condition in Ralph's life that he could not handle.

Like Ralph, there are many people who are disturbed by the fear of not being able to meet their needs throughout life. This serious, insistent worry takes its toll on both mind and body. For most of these people there are only "a few ways out." Very often it's sickness—and sometimes even suicide.

Adults Can Help

Parents and teachers are key people. They have the privilege of helping children and young people develop healthy attitudes toward financial matters.

Children should not be exposed to embarrassment because of low economic status. Neither should they be catered to because their father "owns the town." Adults can point out that greatness does not depend upon finances. Children should learn that many great people have had meager, humble beginnings.

Interestingly enough, the size of a family's bank account does not necessarily determine the attitudes that prevail in the home. Wise parents, whether rich or poor, do not subject their children to needless anxiety about economic security.

True, children must learn the value of money. The sooner they discover that money doesn't "grow on trees," the better off they will be. But when parents place *undue emphasis* on finances, unhealthy attitudes are fostered. The home should not put a premium on the accumulation of money; rather, it should encourage stewardship. Parents should teach children to pray for their needs. When boys and girls are impressed with the fact that God has unlimited resources and always cares for His own, they naturally learn to *trust* instead of *worry*.

Financial pressures visit most families at one time or another. But these need not throw them off balance. In fact, parents can take difficult times and turn them into opportunities to build constructive, positive attitudes toward finances. Two children from different homes, yet with similar financial means, may develop completely *opposite* attitudes toward financial security. The difference? Their parents. One child was give a materialistic outlook. The other received a confident point of view based upon trust in God.

Our Part

We have all heard the saying, "God helps those who help themselves." And this is largely true. God never endorses laziness. He does not intend that we should do nothing, then expect Him to supply our needs. The

Bible tells us that if we do not work, neither should we eat (II Thess. 3:10). We must do our part. And this not only includes earning a living but also wise financial planning.

Wise planning? Indeed! This is just as important as earning power. Thoughtful planning is the oil that makes the wheels of success run smoothly. It prevents us from getting into financial difficulties.

Because we live in a free country, we have the opportunity to do something about our economic security. Most of us have a fairly constant income. Starting with this figure, it's a wise person who sets up a budget. And don't be afraid to do it!

You don't have to be a mathematical genius to develop a workable plan. "Workable" because if you try to follow a budget that is unreasonable, you will only add to your sense of insecurity. Be realistic. Note your fixed expenses—rent or house payments, utilities, food, installment payments. Then allot something *each* month for clothes, medical expenses, insurance, automobile maintenance. Always leave a certain amount for miscellaneous. You'll be glad you did!

Most dedicated Christians set aside at least a tenth of their total income for the Lord's work. This should come first. And it is a good plan to put at least a small amount into a savings account each month.

This is just a rough outline. Each person will want to adapt it to his own needs.

The main thing is to be *realistic*. One young couple I know nearly wrecked their marriage because they were not. Bill was a school teacher. He and his wife, Mary, had been married only a short time when they began to dream about a home of their own. They started saving, and when they thought they had enough money for a down payment, they started looking. Both had come from fine homes and naturally they wanted something nice themselves.

However, they found that new homes in the area

where they wanted to live started at $20,000. Realizing that they could not handle anything that high, they finally settled on a 12-year-old house with a rustic beamed ceiling and two used brick fireplaces. Price: $16,950.

They didn't have enough down payment to qualify for a lower interest FHA loan so they had to use conventional methods. A reputable company loaned $11,950 and after the down payment there was a second trust deed of $3,000 at 6.6 per cent interest. The realty broker said they could pay it off at $25.00 a month with a three-year due date. Payments on the first and second deeds totaled $124.00 a month, not including taxes.

They moved in. And three years moved by all too rapidly. Each year taxes climbed higher until the monthly tax bill alone was $30.00. This meant house payments of $154.00 a month.

Then came the shock. The three-year due date on the second deed was up. They had been paying $25.00 a month on it but some $16.00 of that had gone into interest. They now owed a lump sum of approximately $2,500.

They hadn't been able to save a penny since moving into their home. Now it was almost impossible to refinance the loan. Tension was tight and under the strain Bill developed an ulcer. Mary blamed him for not getting out of the teaching profession and into a job that would provide more money. In time, trouble spread from one area of their marriage to another. The picture wasn't pretty.

Fortunately, before their marriage went completely to pieces, they sat down with pencil and paper and together they did some old-fashioned figuring. For the first time since their marriage they took a realistic attitude toward their present and future economic status.

The problem was so simple that afterward these two

intelligent young people were amazed that they hadn't seen it long before: They sold their house and bought a cheaper one where the total payments, including taxes, were within their budget.

Bill and Mary, however, are not the only ones who have found themselves in this kind of deep water. People are constantly falling into the snare of buying beyond their means. They think they must "keep up with the Jones'." This makes them easy prey for the "easy payment plan." After a while it takes an accountant to keep track of all the payments. And the victims find that they are trapped: there are just *too many* bills to meet. The "easy payments" have become hard ones.

Almost all of us have times when we face difficulties. It is one of the most common problems of mankind. But the measure to which God will bless us depends largely upon how much common sense we use to face the situation realistically and honestly.

God expects us to plan for the future. Remember the story of Pharaoh? God warned him in a dream to save in the time of plenty for the lean years that were to come. The dream went like this: seven fat cattle were devoured by seven lean ones, and seven full ears of corn were consumed by seven thin ears. When Joseph was called upon to interpret this dream, he told Pharaoh that God was warning them to save in the time of their prosperity for the period when famine would visit the land. They did just that. And not only were the people of Egypt spared but they were able to help those who came to them from surrounding countries (Gen. 41).

Should we do less? When God blesses us financially, we need to remember that as His stewards it is our God-given responsibility to use our money wisely. Planning for the future makes sense. And just as God advised Pharaoh to do this, so He would have *us* save for the lean years.

Everyone makes mistakes—we don't always plan

wisely. And when this happens we must be mature enough to face the situation. The first step is to admit our error and ask God's forgiveness. Then we must call upon Him for guidance. Having done this, we are in a position where God can bless us.

God's Part

Although man spends much of his life in quest of security, it is sobering to realize that *there is actually no such thing as absolute financial security*—even for the richest. Any one of a multitude of tragedies may visit a family, leaving it financially destitute. And with the development of atom bombs, hydrogen bombs, cobalt bombs and intercontinental ballistic missiles to carry them, people are brought gravely face to face with the stark fact that their savings will not guarantee them the financial security they had carefully planned.

What then is the answer? Is there no way for man to be economically secure?

No, not on a human level. But this answer is *not* hopeless. We *can* be economically secure—without any threat of failure. How? By committing our lives to the providence of God through His son, Jesus. The Bible tells us that "God shall supply all your need according to His riches in glory by Christ Jesus" (Phil. 4:19).

"All"—"According to *His riches* in glory!" Could anything be more complete? However, we must realize that God promises to supply our "*needs*"—not every whim and selfish desire.

That He "shall supply" is a *guarantee* made by God to His own children. If we trust in Christ as our personal Saviour He forgives us our sins and gives us eternal life. It is then that God becomes our Father. Because He is holy and cannot look upon sin, we must first settle the sin question by asking forgiveness and taking Christ into our lives. Not until then can we claim this "guarantee"; not until then do we have the right to expect His blessings.

God loves His own and He always cares for them. David attested this truth when he said, "I have been young and now am old; yet have I not seen the righteous forsaken, nor his seed begging bread" (Ps. 37:25).

When the Israelites journeyed through the wilderness, God met their needs—not just once, but for the entire forty years. He fed them manna from heaven, gave them water from the rock; and clothed them with garments that did not wear out. "Thy raiment waxed not old upon thee; neither did thy foot swell these forty years" (Deut 8:4). Security? This was it!

And when the multitudes, hungry and weary, thronged about Christ, He did not ignore their physical need. But He took the lunch of a little lad, blessed it and fed them all. Not only did everyone have ample to eat but there was food to spare—twelve baskets full.

God has never ceased caring for those who trust in Him. He is doing it today.

It was during my college days that I became acquainted with a woman who was a living example of this truth. Mrs. Coldwell, a widow with two children, lived near the campus and often invited Christian students into her home for fellowship. This refined, deeply spiritual lady was a great blessing to all of us. She made her humble living by giving music lessons. At times when her pupils were ill and unable to come for lessons, she could not meet her expenses. But Mrs. Coldwell was never defeated—she trusted in a *great* God.

"God knows, and I'm not worrying," she would often say. "Surely He who changed my life, can somehow send in the insignificant sum of thirty dollars."

And God always did!

Years ago, George Mueller, one of England's great Christians and a mighty man of faith, established an orphanage. At times the money ran low and circumstances were trying. But George Mueller believed in prayer and trusted God to meet their needs.

One morning as he and the children sat down for breakfast there was no milk for their cereal. But a small thing like *milk* didn't alter his faith.

"Children," he explained, "although we don't have any milk as yet, we are going to go right ahead and thank God for it just the same. Our Heavenly Father knows about our needs and I am sure He will provide."

Then as they bowed their heads in grateful thanks for something that as yet they did not have, a sudden, loud knock at the door interrupted their prayer.

George stopped praying. "Children," he told them, "this may be God's answer to our prayer."

The door swung open and there stood a milkman. He explained that his wagon had broken down in the street and that he was having to dispose of the milk.

With a smile on his lips, George Mueller lifted his eyes toward heaven and whispered, "Thank You, Lord. I *knew* You would provide."

George Mueller had remarkable faith. But we too can believe God. When we trust Him implicitly, we find a sweet, intimate fellowship which is beyond description. It is then that we find real peace because we are confident that God will not fail us.

Happiness is not dependent upon financial reserves or other types of so-called securities. The happiest people in the world are those who daily trust God to provide their needs, realizing that His storehouse is unlimited and that He cares for them.

Does God care? Enough to be interested in the details of our need? Yes, indeed. Christ said, "Are not two sparrows sold for a farthing? and one of them shall not fall on the ground without your Father. But the very hairs of your head are all numbered. Fear ye not therefore, ye are of more value than many sparrows" (Matt. 10:29-31).

The very hairs of your head are all numbered! Such

detail! Surely, if God is *this* interested in you, He will not neglect your needs. He *wants* to care for you.

If you are a Christian worried about economic security, pour out your heart to God and ask Him to undertake for you. Ask Him to transform your mind so you can see that ultimate security lies not in money but in *Himself*. When He gives you this new transformed attitude, He will flood your heart with peace.

Worry about financial security is like a little stream of fear trickling through the soul. But faith will dry up this annoying stream. Faith and worry do not go together. They cannot both share the same heart or mind. The child of God who believes sincerely that all things work together for his good cannot worry very long. Worry never blesses; it always blights. It upsets digestion and robs of sleep. It makes one irritable. It destroys peace and embitters thinking.

The solution is (1) earnest, daily prayer (2) continual reading of His word and (3) trusting completely that God will not fail. *Prayer and Bible reading build faith.* If we are children of God, let us stop worrying. Why worry when we can *read, pray* and *believe?*

As a child of God we have resources that are hidden to the world. Let us never permit fear of the future to rob us of our joy today.

When we are in the place where God wants us to be, we have no real reason to be concerned about our needs. God promises to provide. With His leading comes His provision. He never separates the two. When we make our own decisions we are on our *own*. But when we follow Him, our present and our future are with God.

Vance Havner, prominent Christian leader, points this out in the story of Elijah, the prophet: "When God told Elijah to go to Cherith and hide there by the brook, He added, 'I have commanded the ravens to feed thee *there*.'

"Later God told Elijah to go to Zerephath and

'dwell *there.*' And added, 'I have commanded a widow woman *there* to sustain thee.' No, He did not promise to feed Elijah just *anywhere*. He did not say, 'Just ramble over the country anywhere you like and I will feed you.' It was limited to *there,* the place of God's will.

"God provides only where He guides. The place of his purpose is the place of His power and His provision. But we must be *there*."

God does provide if we have the right relationship to Him and are obedient to His will. It is sometimes difficult to take the steps of faith necessary for God to reveal His power and wisdom.

Paul and Louise Gates, a young married couple, were meeting their regular monthly expenses when suddenly an emergency came. It demanded considerable money. And they just didn't have that much. For as long as they had been Christians, they had tithed. God had always blessed them. But now an emergency!

"Honey," Paul said to Louise, "what shall we do? If we skip our tithe we can meet our bills. We can make up our tithe later."

"No, Paul," Louise answered. She shook her head as she added, "That wouldn't be right. Our tithe belongs to the Lord *first*. We've always paid our tithe and I don't think we should stop now. I believe that if we honor God and obey Him by paying our debt to Him, He will somehow see us through this financial struggle."

Paul thought a moment. Then stepping over and placing a kiss on his wife's forehead he agreed, "You're right, dear. I'm glad you feel this way about it. We'll pay our tithe as usual and we'll trust the Lord to meet our need."

That evening a friend dropped in to say "hello." After a few minutes he said, "By the way, my wife and I received an unexpected check in the mail the other day. We've prayed about it and we feel led to give a portion of it to you folks. Use it in whatever way you wish."

Paul and Louise looked at each other in utter amazement. How delighted they were—and grateful! When they opened the envelope they saw that the check was made for exactly the amount of their need. God had not failed them. And they were glad that they had not failed Him.

It always pays big dividends to be obedient unto God. The widow of Zarephath is an example of this (I Kings 17:8-16). Things were in a terrible condition—famine and drought in the land. People were dying of hunger every day. Yet, when Elijah came and asked that she prepare him a cake with her last handful of meal and last cup of oil, she was obedient to God. She could have said, "I'm sorry, Elijah, but I'm awfully hard up and I need the food for my own family. Charity begins at home, you know."

How fortunate for her that she did not. Because if she had refused to feed Elijah, she would have been spelling her own doom. She could have saved the meal and the oil for her own use—but after they were gone, she and her son would have starved to death. But because she obeyed God and left her security in His hands, He honored her by continually replenishing the source.

Notice that God did not give her a full year's supply of meal and oil at one time. Instead He met her needs day by day. "And the barrel of meal wasted not, neither did the cruse of oil fail, according to the Word of the Lord" (I Kings 17:16).

So it is today. God may not shower us with large sums of money all at once (although He might), but He does meet our needs as they arise. It is precious this way. We do not become so interested in our financial prosperity that we forget about the Giver. Instead, we trust Him for our "daily bread."

Plan wisely? Yes, prayerfully plan for the future.

But always realize that true economic security stems only from God. He alone knows your needs and is able to provide day by day. "For your heavenly Father knoweth that ye have need of all these things. But seek ye first the kingdom of God, and his righteousness, and *all these things shall be added unto you*" (Matt. 6:32, 33).

Yours is a great God, and the future is safe—*in his hands!*

8

Your Unique Contribution

IT WAS MONDAY morning when Susan Williams spied the postman coming down the street. As she hurried out to meet him he greeted her with, "Good morning, Mrs. Williams. You must be expecting something special."

"Well, I am . . . in a way," Mrs. Williams said.

The postman thumbed through his letters and smilingly handed her one.

"Oh," she said, "it's just the one I was looking for!"

She tore open the envelope and read the letter two lines at a time. "Oh, it's wonderful!" she exclaimed. "They accepted it. They've *really* accepted it!"

"Accepted what?" he asked.

"My song!" she said. "For some time I've been working on a composition, and now a publisher has agreed to publish it."

"Well, isn't that just fine," said the postman. "I didn't know you wrote music."

"Oh, yes," she replied. "I've written many songs but they've never been published. You don't know how I've always wanted to write something that would live on and on—and now my dream has come true!"

Actually, all of us are like Mrs. Williams. Deep down in our hearts is a desire to make some worthwhile contribution to life. Men and women want to be remembered as having given something unique to the world. The engineer dreams of spanning a great gorge —a bridge that will be acclaimed for years after he has gone. The athlete trains arduously to win and set a record. The artist strives for a masterpiece. Parents like to instill into their children thoughts and sayings which will influence generations to come. And who among us hasn't secretly wished that he might write a book? Or even a story? Or perhaps just a poem (if not more than a few lines), which would distinguish us from others?

People everywhere are seeking some magic key that will unlock the door to a more meaningful life. Little wonder then that psychologists and psychiatrists are in general agreement that one of the basic psychological needs of all human beings is to make a worthwhile, unique contribution to life. And unless this need is met, we cannot be our best—physically, emotionally, or spiritually.

How It Affects Us

Dr. Foster knew the Mason family well. One morning when he was out for a walk we passed by the Mason home and noticed Grandma Mason sitting on the porch. "Good morning, Mrs. Mason," he greeted. "How are you feeling?"

"Not so well," she replied.

"Oh no?" the doctor inquired. "What's your trouble?"

"I don't know. I guess I'm just wearing out. Nothing to do. Children all raised and gone. Nothing to occupy my mind. I'm just a burden, I suppose."

As the doctor walked on down the street he kept thinking about Mrs. Mason. *When I see her children,* he thought, *I'll tell them what she needs. Not medicine, but a feeling that she still has a worthwhile place to fill in life.*

The wise doctor wasted no time in getting this message across to the rest of the family. "But what should we do?" they asked. "Grandma isn't strong enough to do any physical work. Anyway, she doesn't need to. We're happy just to have her with us."

"I know," the doctor assured them, "but there are other things she can do."

Then he went on to suggest that they ask her advice on the decisions they make, that they let her know how they count on her prayers.

The Masons took the doctor's advice. And it wasn't long before Grandma began to feel much better. Now she had some real incentives. Out of the wealth of her rich experience she was able to guide and counsel her loved ones and to have a real ministry of prayer. She now felt that she was making a worthwhile contribution. Life took on renewed zest and meaning.

Yes, this is a basic psychological need. We all need to feel that we are contributing something worthwhile. And failure to meet this need is as serious in adulthood as it is in childhood. Such neglect is often reflected in one's physical and mental health. To be happy, to have a dynamic balance amid stress and strain, to be at one's best, each of us needs to feel that day by day he is accomplising something worthwhile. It is important to our personalities, our mental attitudes, and to our physical health.

Boredom is a pitiful thing. It gnaws at the center of our sense of well being. And many people are bored. Bored with routine work. Eight hours a day. Uninspiring job. No challenge. The same thing over and over. Day in and day out. If it isn't a time clock, it is the monotonous task of washing dishes, fixing lunches, washing clothes and cleaning house! It matters not the setting—the routine task is there. And it's drab. Boringly drab.

This is an unhealthy state. Continued boredom warps our personalities. We become sour and uninteresting. To draw the best out of us, we need to be challenged. So the things we do should be significant.

Yes, life without purpose *is* dull. But when we have a goal in life, the world takes on a different perspective. And as the things we do become meaningful, they give us real dynamic. It's the stuff that dreams are made of. And it adds zest and interest to life.

Life Can Be Meaningful

We have all heard the phrase, "Life can be beautiful!" But life can never be beautiful unless it is filled with meaning. This is the difference between significant living and ordinary, empty living.

The world is filled with people who strive to do some "great" thing. But after they achieve their goal—so what? They have made very little contribution to life. Why? Because their goals had little, if any, real significance. The purposes were too flimsy.

One night I attended a meeting of outstanding Christian educators. On my way home I turned on the car radio and tuned in on the news. A newscaster read a "Hollywood bulletin" about a seventeen-year-old screen star who had been awarded a year's contract for nearly one hundred thousand dollars. *What a contrast,* I thought. *The educators are moulding the minds and hearts of our future generations, but this "starlet"—well, what difference does it really make* whether she is *on* or *off* the stage?

To say that there are many important contributions to be made in life would be a gross understatement. The atomic age offers innumerable opportunities for investing our lives and influence. Human resources are sorely needed in every sphere of life. And the world is waiting for men and women who will contribute something significant.

You may have read the delightful book, *The Small Woman,* by Alan Burgess. This is a true story about Gladys Aylward, who at 26 was a parlor-maid in London. She longed to be a missionary to China but she lacked the education to pass the necessary examinations. One night in simple, child-like faith she took all the money she had—two pennies and one halfpenny—and laid it on her open Bible. Then this little parlormaid prayed this sincere prayer: "O God, here's my Bible. Here's my money. Here's me. Use me, God."

And God did!

She arrived in Yangcheng penniless and unable to speak a word of Chinese. The people hated her because she was a foreigner. Even the children cursed her and threw cow dung at her. But Miss Aylward stuck it out and gradually the people began to trust her. She filled a home with orphans and ministered to their pysical needs as she gave them the Gospel. Her witness to our Saviour was so powerful that eventually even some of the proud, old Mandarin of Yangcheng publicly confessed their faith in Jesus Christ.

In a few short years this determined girl had risen from a humble parlor-maid to the exalted position of: Ambassador for Jesus Christ to the People of China.

But there is another side to this business of making a worthwhile contribution in life! For every one that should strike boldly out on a new course like Gladys Aylward, there are thousands who should stay right where they are.

The majority of us may never find life to be a stirring adventure of great deeds. For the most part, life is work. And much of it consists of routine, uninteresting work. Someone has to sack groceries at the market. Someone has to type letters and keep up the office files. Someone has to grease cars. Someone has to work at a drafting board. Someone has to mop kitchen floors.

Escaping from routine jobs is not the answer. Avoiding responsibility doesn't make a person happier.

When psychologists look into case studies they find that many unhappy people skip from job to job and even from town to town. But it seldom solves anything. Because the basic problems are usually not found in the job or the climate, but in the person. So no matter where the people go, their problems are still with them.

The solution then is: Be realistic. An old Latin proverb states it in this way, "A man cannot give what he hasn't got" (*Nil dat quod non habet*). So it is with us. We cannot give the world some great masterpiece of artistry if we do not possess the natural talent. Yes, we can only give what we have. "For unto whomsoever much is given, much shall be required" (Luke 12:48). God does not judge us by how many talents we have: *it is how we use the ones we do have.*

The Bible tells the story of a widow who did not have much to contribute. But she gave all she had and the Lord was pleased. "And Jesus sat over against the treasury . . . and many that were rich cast in much. And there came a certain poor widow and she threw in two mites, which make a farthing. And he called unto him his disciples, and saith unto them. Verily I say unto you, That this poor widow hath cast more in than all they which have cast into the treasury: For all they did cast in of their abundance; but she of her want did cast in all that she had, even all her living" (Mark 12:41-44).

We can't all be big, ostentatious chandeliers in the main lobby. Some of us must light the little back hallway. But the lesser lights make just as significant a contribution as the flashy chandelier. In fact, many times they are needed more.

There is no honest task that can't be done to the glory of God. Brother Lawrence in his classical book of the sixteenth century, *Practicing the Presence of God*, tells how as a cook he was humbly delighted to stir a cake or pick up a straw from the floor for the glory of God.

When we see our station in life through the eyes of a Brother Lawrence we are getting close to the secret of making a genuinely worthwhile contribution in life. "Whether therefore ye eat, or drink, or whatsoever ye do, do all to the glory of God" (I Cor. 10:31).

Do all to the glory of God! What could be a greater challenge! What could be more significant! This means that the most humble job in the world can become a glorious mission for our Saviour. And when we realize this, happiness is at our command.

Never Too Late

It's never too late to start doing something worthwhile.

Like the story of Mae Watson. From the time she was just a little girl, she had wanted to be an educator. She enjoyed children and had a real gift for teaching. But circumstances had kept her from attending college.

The years had passed all too quickly. And Mae became more and more dissatisfied with her routine office job. "I want to work with people," she said. "I want to help children."

Then one day she shocked all her friends. She left her desk and headed for college. "But Mae," her friends suggested, "aren't you a little *old* for college?"

"No," was Mae's plucky answer. "Of course, I may be older than the rest of the students. But I can't start any younger. And the longer I delay, the older I'll be."

So Mae started college. She soon discovered that age made little difference. The four years flew by. When she stepped up for her diploma she knew it had been well worth the effort.

There are many people like Mae. Sometimes it takes courage to step out of a rut, but it is always gratifying when you head toward your goal—no matter what your age.

In Southern California there is a fine Christian high school, Culter Academy, that was founded years ago by Mabel Culter. In 1954 Miss Culter, age 60, decided that being the president of a noted Christian school was fine, but that there were other pressing needs in the world.

She confided to her friends that she wanted to be a missionary to Korea!

"What?" they thought, "she can't really *mean* it—not at *her* age."

Her friends tried to persuade her that she was needed at the academy. ('They were too polite to tell her that she was simply "too old" for any mission board to accept). But their discouragement could not hold back Mabel Culter. She knew what she wanted and she went after it. Sixty? It did not bother her in the least. She applied to the Evangelical Alliance Mission (TEAM) and explained that her experience was just what was needed. And to the surprise of everyone, the mission board agreed. So off to Korea she flew to help establish an orphanage, a hospital and a Bible institute!

The quality of a person's contribution in life does not depend on age. True, youth has vigor. But maturity has the advantage of experience. Challenges are for those who accept them. God does not limit the applicants to a certain age bracket. It is never too late to do the job if God is calling you to it.

Encouraging Others

The greatest joys in life come as we invest ourselves in others. And every day offers an opportunity to do this—especially through encouraging those around us. The difference between a man who makes a significant, worthwhile contribution in life and the man who does not, is often one word: "encouragement." The Bible says that "Where there is no vision, the people perish . . ." (Prov. 29:18).

It might be a boy down the street, a lady at church, the man at the office or a husband or wife. But "big things" hinge largely on encouragement.

Discouragement may attack anyone. When things go wrong a person may think, "I might as well give up." But your word of encouragement will give him a new impetus.

Many people do not know their potential. It often takes that extra little "boost" to get the ball rolling. There are people with real ability who never do anything about it. Why? Because they need someone to give them confidence—they need to know others believe in them.

John is a good example. After high school he started driving a truck for a local firm. But a neighbor realized that John had a lot to offer and that he could be making a much greater contribution to life if he had the training. So one day the neighbor had a long talk with John. He encouraged him to enroll in college the next semester.

John did. Engineering was his choice. And several years later John graduated and joined a large equipment firm.

It wasn't long before he started working on a special project of his own. And in a few years John had perfected it—an important piece of heavy-duty earth moving equipment. Roadbuilders everywhere began to use it. And before long many more motorists were enjoying big, new highways.

Now John was making a significant contribution to society. But little did people realize that the man responsible for this was the "neighbor" who had encouraged a teen-age truck driver to do something worthwhile.

Contributing for Eternity

Billy Graham has repeatedly said that without the prayers of faithful believers his campaigns would be monumental failures. And this is true of all Christian activity. Spritual work is energized by the Holy Spirit. Christians who fail to pray, fail to make one of their great contributions. Think of the contribution you make when you daily remember your pastor at the throne of grace. Think of the contribution you make when you pray for that missionary in some difficult place of the world. Think of the contribution you make when you pray for that loved one who has not yet come to the Savior.

In God's Word we are admonished to pray: "Confess

your faults one to another, and pray one for another, that ye may be healed. The effectual fervent prayer of a righteous man availeth much" (James 5:16).

Some people feel that because of ill health or family obligations, they cannot contribute much to the work of the Lord. But they can. Any believer can enter into God's holy presence and pray. And prayer changes things—and people. Some of the greatest prayer warriors that this world has ever known have been crippled with disease and broken in body. Martha Snell Nicholson, for example, suffered years from numerous infirmities. Yet her life was radiant because she kept in constant contact with God through prayer. This dear woman was an inspiration and a blessing to countless thousands.

Do the cares of the home interfere? Then consider Susannah Wesley. She had nineteen children. Besides caring for her large family, she gave all of the children their educational training, teaching them herself. A busy woman? That's stating it mildly. But she was never too busy to pray. She prayed every day with each one of the children individually, besides praying for them alone. But it was worth it. Her prayers produced two mighty men of God that stirred all of Great Britain. Hers was a great contribution through prayer —and the names of her sons, John and Charles Wesley, stand as a towering tribute to their praying mother.

Another eternal contribution in life is that of *giving*. Churches could not preach the Gospel, Christian colleges and Bible schools could not train future leaders, gospel broadcasts could not go out over the air, if humble believers did not give. There would be few missionaries on the foreign fields if Christians did not give. When God's people give their money to further the Gospel, they are investing in *eternal souls*. Such contributions are so great that they cannot be measured.

I once heard a man say that the most annoying part of being a Christian was receiving appeals for donations. "It seems as though every Christian organization in the world is out after your money," he said.

I thought to myself, *Giving is one of the greatest joys of being a Christian. It is a privilege.* Each month my wife and I look forward to giving our tithes and offerings to various Christian organizations. Naturally we cannot give to every need, but it is a wonderful blessing to help the ones that God has placed upon our hearts.

When a person gives of his income, it represents his talent, his time, his earning power and his thinking. In short, when a person gives his money, in a sense he gives *himself*.

Most of us realize that "the harvest truly is plenteous, but the laborers are few" (Matt. 9:37). But it is also true that the *money is scarce*. Missionary leaders have told me that the greatest barrier to reaching unevangelized areas is not personnel—it is lack of *finances*. There are young people applying to mission boards today who may never be sent out. Why? Simply because there is no money to send them!

Not everyone is privileged to become a missionary. And few of us have the opportunity to reach the millions by radio. But we can all be on the team. How? By systematically tithing our income and giving our offerings unto the Lord. In this way, our money will have lasting value because we have invested for eternity.

Money isn't the only commodity we can give, however. Our time and our talent is just as valuable—and sometimes more so. When we give generously of our time, our training and our ability, we invest ourselves.

Our time. This is a precious item. And a personal one. The moments are here—and then they are gone forever. But we are held responsible for how these moments are used. God tells us to "redeem the time" —to take advantage of every minute. There is no better way to do this than to offer our time to God. Perhaps God wants you to spend time visiting the sick.

He may want you to open your home for a Bible class, or sew clothing for a missionary orphanage. Whatever it may be, time given to the Lord is time gained.

And our talents. Christ tells us not to "hide our light under a bushel" (Matt. 5:15). Since God has endowed us with every ability we have, we should use it for His glory. Perhaps it may be singing in the choir, or doing children's work, or counseling with young people. Whatever your talent is, develop it and use it for the Lord. This is your contribution—individually and *personally yours*.

Our belongings should also be dedicated to the Lord. When our home, our car, yes, everything we own is surrendered to the Lord, He can and will use them for His glory. Our temporal possessions then become implements of spiritual blessing.

God calls some of us into full-time Christian work. This is an honor and a sacred trust. When God calls us to some specific task, we dare not let it go unheeded. We *must* obey if we are to be effective Christians.

As we walk close to the Lord and to His will, He makes us channels of blessing. It is only then that we make a lasting contribution—one that will count for eternity.

The Greatest Contribution

Children are always talking about what they are going to be when they "grow up." A nurse, a fireman, a circus clown! And as they reach adolescence, the picture begins to take more form. They realize that it is a decision they must eventually make. When they pass through their "turbulent teens" they spend more and more time thinking about how they might use their lives. Dr. Henrietta Mears, noted Christian leader, has often said, "The paramount issue with every young adult is, 'What am I going to do with my life?' "

It is only natural that we should want to know what

our greatest contribution in life might be. And we *can* know.

To learn the answer, we must turn to God's Word, the Bible. There we see that the most precious commodity is *life itself*. God says that a person's soul (the life that lives on forever) is worth more than the whole world, and that there is nothing valuable enough to give in exchange for it (Mark 8:36).

God also says that nothing is more important than the salvation of a soul. Nothing, absolutely nothing can compare with leading someone to Christ. The proportions of this contribution are so great that they are measured not in time, but in eternity. To save a soul from hell, from a Christless eternity; to point him to the matchless Saviour who alone can satisfy on earth, and enable him to abide in heaven for endless ages—this, through the work of the Holy Spirit, is *the greatest contribution of which any human being is capable!*

In His Word, God has said, "He that winneth souls is wise." Every Christian can be actively engaged in soul winning. It is only reasonable to believe that God who has given us the desire to make a worthwhile contribution in life, also enables us to fulfill it.

Years ago in the city of Boston there lived an "insignificant" man by the name of Ed Kimball. Among other things, Kimball was a Sunday school teacher who realized that the greatest contribution he could make was not just to earn a living but to tell others about the saving power of Christ. So he kept witnessing to the boys in his class. Among them was a young shoe salesman, Dwight L. Moody. Every week Ed Kimball made it a point to visit him and talk to him about his soul. In time, Moody surrendered his heart to Christ.

Kimball's evangelism did not end there. He had touched a firebrand for Christ who was to be heard " 'round the world." Thousands upon thousands learned about his wonderful Saviour, the Lord Jesus

Christ. In fact, today D. L. Moody is known as the man who shook two continents with the Gospel of Jesus Christ. What a great contribution Kimball made when he reached this "giant" for Christ.

Another example is Steve Landon. At eighteen he was one of the roughest, toughest, football players that ever hit Washington High. Standing a little over six feet tall, he weighed 195 pounds and was every inch a man.

"How does he manage to stay in school?" people asked. "He breaks every rule in the book and he's not always sober when he arrives on the campus."

One Monday morning everything came to a climax. Steve had been drinking the night before. After a big family fight he stumbled to school ready to "whip the world."

Miss Barkley, his English teacher, greeted him as he made his appearance in the school library. She had always taken an interest in Steve. But Steve wasn't in the mood to talk to anyone. Sensing that Steve was in serious trouble, she followed him over to his locker. "It's no use talking to me," Steve snapped at Miss Barkley. "I've got my own life to live and I'm going to live it just the way I please."

Throughout the day Miss Barkley kept praying for Steve. *They're sure to expel him this time*, she thought. And they did.

That evening she called Steve on the phone and asked him to come over to her house. If ever he needed a friend, it was then. So Steve went over to see Miss Barkley.

She told him more about Christ and how He had died for people like Steve. She told him that he could have real happiness if he would only surrender his heart to Him. Then she invited him to go with her to hear an evangelist who was coming to speak at the city auditorium. Steve promised that he would go. A few nights later the service began with a packed house.

And Steve was there—slouched down in the very last row of the auditorium.

The evangelist brought a powerful message. And the Spirit of God touched hearts. At the end of the service Steve headed for the altar. "I felt," he said, "that I couldn't get there fast enough. I talked with a counselor after the meeting and right then and there I settled the whole thing. I told the Lord that from now on I was going to live for Him—and I never meant anything more seriously in my life."

That was the turning point for Steve. Miss Barkley helped to get him reinstated in high school. And this time things were different. It wasn't long until graduation. Then, on to university. Steve stayed true to the Lord all through his college days. A few years later he became an outstanding youth leader in his area. Today, young people are thrilled as they hear this fine young man of God give his testimony of how a high school teacher talked with him, befriended him, prayed for him and counseled with him until he came to know Christ as his personal Saviour.

It was true that Miss Barkley was making a worthwhile contribution as an English teacher. But she realized that there was an even greater contribution to be made. To her, the structure of a sentence was not nearly as important as the salvation of a soul. And although she did not neglect her job as a teacher, neither did she neglect her duty as a Christian. Grammar? Yes, she taught it. But even more than that, she influenced young people for God.

Preachers have no monopoly on giving out the Gospel. They do not have the "exclusive" on winning souls for Christ. That means that every Christian can have a part in making this "greatest" contribution. In fact, it is his responsibility.

Christ tells us, "Ye shall be witnesses unto me both in Jerusalem, and in all Judaea, and in Samaria, and unto the uttermost part of the earth" (Acts 1:18). We cannot all go to the *uttermost part of the earth,* but we can make certain that we cover the home base—our own "Jerusalem." It may be a business associate to whom we should witness, or the lady next door. Or perhaps we should speak to that classmate at school, or give a tract to the mailman. There are countless ways to witness effectively if our eyes are open to our God-given opportunities. Our "mission field" often consists of those with whom we work and play and do business. They are *ours* to win. You have heard it often, but it is nonetheless true: "Everyone knows someone else." Our immediate responsibility then is to those with whom we rub shoulders.

It was a pal who reached Jack for Christ. Jack was a New York boy. But that wasn't unusual, because there were thousands of young men living in New York City. Like most of the other fellows in his crowd, Jack was interested in everything that was going on—everything except his soul's salvation.

Jack's best friend was George Schilling. Both of these fellows played trombones in a jazz band and in the United States Cavalry. Out for a good time? Yes, and in a worldly sense, they usually had it!

But something happened to George. One night he walked into a downtown church in New York City where they were holding a New Year's Eve Watch Night service. That was the night for George. During the service Dr. Will Houghton brought a stirring gospel message, and when the invitation was given to accept Christ, George Schilling was the first to walk down the aisle. And he meant business. That night as George walked out of the church he was determined to live for the Lord.

Shortly afterward he talked to his pal, Jack, about how Christ had come into his heart. Jack was puzzled. This didn't sound like George. One night George gave him a New Testament. Jack was too polite to refuse it.

But before he reached home he tore it up and threw it away. None of that "sissy stuff" for him.

But George did not give up. He continued to witness to Jack and six months later they went off to army camp togther.

In this tough army crowd, thought Jack, *George will forget all about his religion. I know what George used to be and I'm sure he can't hold out.*

That didn't happen. George was man enough to stand up for Christ. Jack watched his buddy for full two weeks—watched him like a hawk twenty-four hours a day as they lived and worked in that army camp. Jack was amazed at the marvelous change in his friend's life. "George has something worth having," Jack decided. But still he did not give his heart to Christ.

A few weeks later when they had come back home, George persuaded Jack to attend an evangelistic service by asking him to play his trombone. Jack loved to play, so he went. But he was miserable. Although he did not make a decision when the evangelist gave the invitation, Jack couldn't get away from the pull of the Gospel. That night, alone in his room, he knelt by his bed and gave his heart to the Saviour.

The story doesn't end there, however. Jack knew that his main job in life was to witness for Christ. And he started right in doing it. A few years later Jack had to leave his regular employment because he was getting "too many invitations to speak for the Lord."

The years passed and through Jack's preaching and radio ministry many thousands have found Christ as their personal Saviour. The Lord led Jack Wyrtzen to establish several camps in the United States as well as in foreign countries, where young and old come to hear the Gospel. In addition, God has led Jack to help support over sixty missionaries throughout the world.

George Schilling, the young man who led Jack Wyrtzen to Christ, could have used his time doing many other things. But he realized that the greatest contribution that one could ever make was to win a soul to Christ. So George was faithful. And through his consistent witness, Jack Wyrtzen found the Lord.

How about you? Are you making the maximum contribution in life? Or are you allowing the *good* to rob you of the *best*?

There are learned *educators* who have earned advanced degrees and who understand the psychology of learning. They have amassed great stores of information. They have devoted themselves to teaching mankind. Making a great contribution? Yes, but not enough. Since they have never come to know the Truth, Christ the Son of God, they cannot impart godly wisdom to their students.

There are *medical doctors* who have devoted years to specialized study of the human body. They understand much about anatomy, bodily functions, disease and the science of healing. And they are making a contribution to society. But they do not go far enough. They know nothing of the Great Physician who heals the soul. And they are unable to show their patients how to put on incorruption, how to have eternal life.

There are brilliant *psychologists* who can give an array of psychological tests to diagnose the causes of maladjustments. They can evaluate the human intellect and can detect the workings of the mind. But they fail to give their clients the "Mind of Christ."

There are well informed *attorneys* who can advise their clients about intricate details of national and international law. But because they are helpless to explain the law of God that converts the soul, the contribution they make is a limited one.

There are top *men of science* who help mankind "get off the ground"—to find their way to the moon. Yet they are helpless to point a man to heaven.

There are clever *salesmen* who can explain the advantage of their product and convince people of the superiority of their wares. Yet they fail to show the advantage of the glorious Gospel—they cannot persuade people to accept the gift of God.

There are skilled *craftsmen* who build with utmost precision. But they fail to build a life for God.

There are artistic *homemakers* who understand how to beautify the home. They excel in the art of flower decoration, color design, furniture arrangement, and many other aspects of home management. And yet they forget the beauty of the soul; they completely neglect the beauty of holiness.

There are even *ministers* who present oratorical sermons—telling people "How to face life." And yet they never tell people how they can have *eternal* life—how they can face *both life and death.*

The contributions of men are worthy. It is right that we should help our fellow man. But unless we make the *greatest* contribution, we do not go far enough. For it is not until we help lead people to the Saviour that we can serve humanity on the highest level—the divine.

It is not just a matter of contributing if we feel like it. It is not like donating to charity. God's work is urgent. It cannot be turned aside. Since God is not willing that any should perish (II Peter 3:9), it is our responsibility to reach the unsaved with the Gospel.

If we are not working members of the team, we are missing out on the blessing. What can we do? We can give our time, talent and resources, and we can witness. We can study so that we will be ready to give an answer for the hope that is in us (I Peter 3:15). Some us will sow, others will water, and still others will reap. It matters little what part of the job is assigned to us. The important question is: Are we faithful in doing it?

The work of our hands will not endure. The great buildings that stand as proud monuments to our civilization will some day deteriorate and crumble. As durable as they are, stone and steel are not indestructible. The mighty bridges that span great waterways will some day fall into the abyss below. Scientific theories are ever changing. The great discoveries of today will be obsolete tomorrow.

Nothing we can do on a human level is permanent. The sound of our song will grow faint; the masterpiece we paint will fade; the books that we write will yellow and be forgotten. Our silver and gold that we have worked so hard to accumulate will tarnish. And this body that we carefully nurture and adorn will eventually lie in the grave.

Only when we deal with eternity can we expect the results to be immortal. So it is that there is *one* contribution man can make that will be of *lasting* value. Yes, the souls that we win for Christ will live on forever and ever. And through eons to come, those whom we have brought to the Lord will stand as a living memorial to our contribution here on earth.

True, one of man's basic drives is to make a worthwhile contribution in life. But the greatest contribution of all—the only one that will stand through eternity—is to have a part in bringing an immortal soul into the kingdom of God. This, indeed, is the way to genuine happiness.

9

Secrets of Success

WHEN I WAS a young boy I heard a neighbor say, "If a man's not a success by the time he's thirty-five, he'll never be one."

Immediately I perked up my ears. Not only did I swallow his statement but I supposed success was measured by wealth.

Years later I discovered that this was not true. No, it wasn't that this well-meaning neighbor had deliberately told a falsehood. He was sincere but he did not know the facts.

Actually, there is no age beyond which one can say, "He'll never be successful." Furthermore, contrary to what many people think, true success has very little to do with the size of a man's bank roll. But success and achievement *are* important—highly important. In fact, they are vital to our physical and mental health. Success draws the best out of a man and in return, it tends to fill him with normal, healthy attitudes. The result—a well adjusted person.

TONIC FOR YOUR PERSONALITY

Success is the tonic that puts zest into living—the "pay-off" for our efforts. That is why people who have never moved forward in life are seldom happy. They are suffering from an undernourished incentive—a malady that takes its toll in personality. People develop into interesting individuals as they achieve. And when they are *not* progressing, the results are bound to be detrimental.

Marie was an example of a person who was suffering from a "standstill." Due to unfortunate circumstances in her family, she had to leave high school and look for a job. In the community where she lived, employment was limited. So she took the only thing available, a filing job in a small office. Marie liked music and in this field she had unusual potential. But without training or experience her talent was held captive. Filing, filing, filing! How she hated it. This was not success and she knew it. Naturally, it reflected in her personality. No zest, little happiness, and constant conflict.

Nothing is more pitiful than the person who is standing still or going backward. His life is like stagnant water, unhealthy and undesirable. Stagnant water is motionless—has no outlet or source of refilling. And when people become inactive and are not taking in or giving out, they too become stagnant.

On the other hand, no one is more *interesting* and more vital than the person who is moving forward. Man was made to go forward, not backward. We grow, we develop, we mature. And as we progress, our personalities take on a vibrant sparkle. Progress is basic to all life: it is essential to every human being.

What happens to a person who continually fails? He becomes discouraged, taking the defeatest attitude of "Why try? I can't win anyway." There is nothing much more uninspiring and uninteresting than this kind of "wet blanket." He is likely to become suspicious, blaming people and circumstances for his lack of success. In short, he is extremely hard to live with because he has never found his "niche" in life. It is not uncommon for a person like this to complain of headaches and nervousness or other symptoms of emotional disturbance. Little wonder, then, that psychiatrists and psychologists agree that this basic psychological need, that of being successful, must be met if a person is to be his best.

In contrast to those who have not encountered much success, we find that people who are meeting with at least a measure of success in life are more likely to be interesting. They are usually optimistic and inspirational. Successful people look forward to the future. Why? Because the past has been profitable and the present is encouraging. As a result, they face tomorrow with confidence! When a person is achieving success, circumstances are not a threat to him. He has been able to overcome obstacles in the past so naturally, he is *not* afraid of the future. Is it any wonder then, that people who are successful are easier to associate with than those who are failures?

Think of the people you know! In the office—that griper, always complaining about one thing or another. You can be almost certain he is not the vice-president of the concern; more than likely, he's a discouraged clerk who has been sitting at the same desk doing the same routine job for the past twenty years. And in school—it is usually not the "A" student who grumbles about too much home work and too strict discipline. In church—well, it's the same story. A person who is being used of God doesn't spend his time finding fault with the preacher or criticizing the deacons and elders. He's too busy doing something worthwhile. So it is that as we experience at least some success, our personalities improve and we become enriched, interesting individuals who are better able to get along with others.

SUCCESS MEANS MORE SUCCESS

Success *is* the basis for greater accomplishments. For when we succeed at little things we continue to succeed at bigger ones. Even the smallest success prepares us for further achievement.

You have heard the old adage, "Success is a ladder and those who attain must start at the bottom and climb to the top." Shopworn as this statement is, it carries a lot of truth. Each step up prepares you for the next rung. When you take one successful step, you look forward to the next—and the next—and the next. When most of your tries are successes, you can *take* a few bumps and bruises along the way. But when the failures outweigh the successes, it spells one thing —discouragement! And discouragement often breeds more trouble.

This is true of both young and old. Parents notice it. Teachers notice it, and so do employers.

I remember Sandra, a fourth grade girl who had been referred to me for special study. On her referral sheet, the teacher wrote, "I'm wondering if she's just lazy." When I observed the girl in the classroom, I readily saw that she was not interested in her school work. That afternoon I gave her a psychological examination and found that her intelligence was only low average. After studying her school records, visiting with her parents and talking with her former teachers, I felt that I had uncovered the roots of her difficulty. Sandra was not ready for the work that was being presented in her class. I was certain that her biggest problem was discouragement. She had run into it for years—both at home and school.

When I talked with the teacher, I suggested that she give Sandra work appropriate to her ability. We discussed ways in which the teacher could encourage her. Together we planned many ways to help Sandra achieve a degree of success.

A month or so later I saw the teacher again. "Do you remember Sandra?" she asked. "Well, she's doing much better. Her school work is improving. But even more than that, her whole attitude is different."

Like everyone else, Sandra thrived on encouragement. She had a basic psychological need—that of experiencing success and achievement. As soon as that need was met, she felt encouraged and happy. Now, for a change, she was meeting with some success. She was no longer a problem girl. Why? Because she had a new self concept. No longer did she think of herself as a "dunce." She had a new role—success.

It's not easy to be enthusiastic about the future when one has not been successful in the past. Failure dims our outlook. Tomorrows seldom look bright if our yesterdays have been marred by dissatisfaction. This was impressed upon me one summer when I joined Dr. Leo Phearman, an outstanding reading specialist, to conduct a reading clinic for boys and girls. These ten to fourteen-year-old children had at least average intelligence, yet they had never learned to read. By now they were so discouraged that they felt there was no hope for them. One of our biggest tasks was to convince them that they *could succeed.* Once this spark of hope had been fanned back to life, these youngsters were on the road to real progress.

There's nothing like failure to kill incentive and ambition. People don't mind working hard when the reward is accomplishment. But to work without results is no better than aimlessly marking time—going 'round and 'round in the same old rut, getting nowhere. Like a donkey on a treadmill. And that's when life becomes the "same old grind."

Yes, it takes more than *striving* to develop a well adjusted personality. It also takes some *arriving.*

Success and Health

Lois and her husband sat in my office one evening and told me their story. They had been on the mission field only a short time when she became ill. She seemed to lose all interest in life. Unable to sleep or eat, she lost considerable weight. Doctors on the field urged her husband to fly her back to America immediately.

After the young couple returned home, other medical doctors examined her, but found no serious physical causes of her breakdown. They advised her to get psychological help.

During the months that I worked with Lois she gained real insight into many of the causes of her illness. She had been raised in a family that was dominated by an older sister and by an unduly critical father. Lois' sister was not only competent; she was aggressive. Lois was made to feel that she could not do anything as well as her sister. Her father was always quick to criticize. "It's not good," he would say, "for children to get a big head." He believed that the best way to get them to improve was to point out how they should have done better.

The result? Lois grew up feeling dependent and inferior. She thought she was not capable of meeting things on her own. Although she accepted Christ as her personal Saviour a few years before leaving for the mission field, the more than twenty years of injurious experiences had caused profound damage. There were traces of these personality characteristics before she left America, but they did not become so dramatically apparent until she reached the foreign field. There Lois was exposed to undue stress and strain in a strange, lonely land where unusual hardships faced her every day. And to make matters worse, there was no one with whom she felt free enough to talk this thing out and to share her terrible feelings of depression. Naturally, the extreme emotional conditions that had prevailed through the years brought serious physical reactions so that she was finally unable to go on.

Through Christian psychological help and medical attention, Lois grew steadily better until she was able to carry on her regular duties in the home, then return to the field. But what a terrible price to pay for a needless experience! Yes, her parents had provided for her financial and physical needs—she had a nice home, nourishing food and good clothes. But she lacked that important element of success and achievement!

It takes more than fresh air and vitamins to keep a person healthy—a good emotional climate is needed too. Psychologists and psychiatrists continually re-emphasize the close relationship between the physical and the emotional—one affects the other. Since this is true, it is easily understood how success is basic to our well being.

The successful person is usually confident and he faces life with a wholesome mental attitude. He has a sound, emotional outlook and is not easily upset by disturbances. Because he has overcome other problems in the past, he is not overly concerned when new hurdles arise. This, in turn, directly relates to his physical condition. When a person runs into constant discouragement and defeat, it is injurious to his health. When failure continually operates in an individual's life, it can disrupt the body's glandular balance and cause headaches, backaches and many other physical ailments. Success then, at least to some extent, is essential if a person is to maintain good health—both mental and physical.

One day Mr. Burton came to my office. His face wore a tired, haggard expression. His whole attitude and bearing was one of dejection and defeat.

"I don't know what's the matter with me, Dr. Narramore," he confided, slumping down into a chair, "but everything seems to be wrong."

Then Mr. Burton told me his story. He had been a Christian for a number of years, had a fine wife and two lovely daughters. It would seem that he had everything to make him happy—but yet he was *miserable*.

"I'm *so* discouraged," he confessed. "I don't want to be like this but I'm terribly unhappy. I'm just a big failure, I guess."

He went on to tell me how dissatisfied he was—on the job, at home, in his church, yes, everywhere. And to him, life was intolerably dull.

"I'm tired all the time and I just don't feel well," Mr. Burton continued. "Yet when I went to our family doctor and had a complete physical check-up, he could find nothing wrong. But something *is* wrong. And whatever it is, I do hope you can help me find my trouble."

Poor health? Yes, but not from a physical cause.

As I talked with Mr. Burton I soon sensed that he was a brilliant man but was working at a job that almost anyone with no education could handle. Men with far less ability than he, were giving him orders all day. And in his particular company there was nothing he could do about it.

In the ensuing visits I gave him an intellectual examination and found that his intelligence was not only high but in the gifted class. After giving him several vocational aptitude tests we discovered that he had special ability in *several* lines for which he had no training or experience.

I encouraged him to start night school, and if possible, get a leave of absence from his work so he could take some summer work at a nearby university. He did this, and after two years he moved to a new company and into a position, for which he had unusual talent. Here he was able to utilize his recent training. Within a short time he gained recognition in his office, and a little later he was given a top executive position.

His poor mental health had disappeared. Now he was radiantly happy at home, at work, and at church. Success made the difference.

WE CAN HELP

Have you ever thought how much success depends upon our attitudes toward each other? When those around us recognize and encourage us, life is a place of satisfaction and success. When they do not, it is more than likely to be a place of defeat and failure.

Take Mr. Lane and Mr. Black, for example. They lived on the same street, had similar jobs, and both had small families.

But the similarity ended there. If you had known them personally, you would have realized a great difference between the two. Lane felt successful, but Black didn't. The difference? In their cases, it was due to their wives.

Mrs. Lane took nearly every opportunity to encourage her husband and to give him recognition. "Our Daddy is the best in the world," she would tell her children. "We love him, don't we!"

Then turning to her husband she would admiringly say, "Honey, you're just wonderful."

On the other hand, Mrs. Black seemed to take her husband for granted. Love him? Yes, undoubtedly; but she constantly pointed out to him the things they *didn't* have and the things they needed. She failed to give him the daily recognition that helps keep a man happy and healthy—the feeling that he is at least fairly successful.

After a number of years the two women had left permanent imprints on their husbands—one of success, the other, defeat.

We can't deny that recognition and status *are* important, not only in our marriage relationships, but in all phases of life. Children and adults alike need to feel that they are successful. At home—at school—at church—in the office—wherever we live, work or play, being successful is an important factor. We can help our children, our friends and our relatives feel that they are successful by our encouragement and support.

Yes, we *do* have a responsibility. But more than that, we have the joy of encouraging and recognizing others. When we let people know that we have confidence in them, we give them the "boost" that makes them feel successful. The by-products: good physical and mental health on their part and more happiness on ours. Consequently, success is not measured by some mythical yardstick. Rather, it is counted in terms of the recognition we receive from our friends, and the recognition we give to them!

Successful Fools

That a person can be successful and still be a fool is a paradox. But unfortunately, it's quite possible—and even more sadly, a common truth.

I'm thinking of a certain man who "made good" financially. In fact, he was wealthy. He had worked hard through the years and had made his fortune as a farmer. Everyone considered him a highly successful man and he prided himself on his own achievements.

One day as he was looking over his property and his belongings, he realized that he had more possessions than he had storage room. So he came up with a plan for expansion and proposed to pull down his barns and build greater ones where he could put all his fruits and his goods.

He smiled with evident satisfaction as he decided that he would now retire. "Soul," he told himself, "thou hast much goods laid up for many years; take thine ease, eat, drink, and be merry."

But God said unto him, "Thou fool, this night thy soul shall be required of thee: then whose shall those things be which thou hast provided?"

Fool? Yes, indeed! A fool because he was so shortsighted. He hadn't planned beyond the brief span of this life. And he hadn't reckoned with eternity or the fact that God holds the future in His almighty hand.

God tells us that "a man's life consisteth *not* in the abundance of the things which he possesseth" (Luke 12:15). But this man evidently did not know that. He had a wrong, an earthly sense of values.

The story of this "successful fool" is recorded in the Bible (Luke 12:16-21). Unfortunately, there have been thousands—yes, millions just like him. Today, as it has been through the ages, people are more *materialistic* than ever. They measure their successes by the false yardsticks of materialism and power.

"You can't take it with you," is more than a time-worn adage. It is a nugget of truth that we need to consider carefully. Not long ago two men were discussing a mutual acquaintance who had passed away. "How much did he leave?" asked one. "Everything!" replied the other.

How true this is. We leave *everything* we accumulate here on this earth. That is why God warns us to "lay not up for yourselves treasures upon earth, where moth and rust doth corrupt, and where thieves break through and steal: But lay up for yourselves treasures in heaven, where neither moth nor rust doth corrupt, and where thieves do not break through nor steal: For where your treasure is, there will your heart be, also" (Matt. 6:19-21).

Sometimes we may experience financial reverses or meet with trying circumstances. But to Christians, these losses are not too disturbing, because their treasures are laid up in heaven. Compared to the celestial glory of these riches, earthly treasures look insignificant and puny. And they are.

Yet there are countless numbers of people who foolishly stake their entire future on a mirage. Fortune? Fame? Love? Reputation? Are these the elements of success? Not really, because this kind of success is only on the surface. And when it crumbles, people's dreams crash with it.

Many have climbed to the top of their rainbows and have reached their pots of gold—popular acclaim, wealth, or other achievements. But once having reached this much sought goal, they still are dissatisfied and extremely unhappy. Why? Because they have left God out of their plans. Success obtained without the blessing of God is a farce—shallow and empty. And in God's sight, it's worthless. "For what shall it profit a man if he gain the whole world, and lose his own soul?" (Mark 8:36).

The Road to Success

The first essential on the road to success is to *start* right—*to put first things first.*

The very first verse of the Bible reads, "In the *beginning* God" (Gen. 1:1). Have you had a beginning with God? It's the only authentic starting place. God tells us to "seek ye *first* the kingdom of God and His righteousness; and all these things shall be *added* unto you" (Matt. 6:33).

So it is that the first step to success is found in accepting Christ as one's personal Saviour—coming to God as a repentant sinner and trusting completely in the work that Christ accomplished on the Cross for our salvation. When you have started on God's road, you have started on the road to true success. It's solid and it's sure All other roads are treacherous, because no matter how great your success may be in this world, you will be doomed to eternal failure in the next.

People write books and give lectures on how to be successful. Yet, they often leave out the most basic element of all. Real success cannot be achieved anywhere but in the center of God's will. Some may appear to be achieving success but when we view them from God's perspective, we see that these people are really on little side lines and are not even in the running at all.

All ambitions, except one, end with life. They are only for the duration of human existence. The workman must lay aside his tools; the writer his pen; the surgeon his knife; the astronomer his telescope; the explorer his chart; the scientist his tube and acids; the musician his song.

God tells us that "the world passeth away, and the lust thereof: but he that doeth the will of God abideth forever" (I John 2:17). So it is that only one ambition will last for all eternity, only one ambition will demand all the ages for its perfect realization.

In the Old Testament it was said of King Uzziah that "as long as he sought the Lord, God made him to prosper." This is also true of us. As Christians we cannot expect to prosper unless each day is marked by sincere consecration.

But remember, success is never *dumped* into a person's lap. God gave us brains and brawn and He expects us to put them to use. So success also requires *action.* God expects us to do our part—to pray and to read His Word—and then to *work* in obedience to His will. Many people are not as successful in life as they might be because they are in the wrong vocation or profession. But here again, our relationship to God is significant. When we know Christ, He gives us new ambitions and desires. He guides us into the work He has chosen for us and for which we have ability. He graciously opens certain doors and closes others to insure our success. Actually, when God is directing our paths, we cannot fail! And God makes no mistakes.

I knew a teen-aged girl named Gloria. She was vivacious and pretty and her ambition in life was to become an actress and star in the theatre.

"Oh, Dr. Narramore," she sighed, "I can't think of anything more fabulous than to be a movie star. It's so glamorous and all. I *do* hope I have enough talent."

We talked for a little while about her plans and her ambitions, and I took the opportunity to tell her what Christ wanted to do in her life. She listened intently and tears filled her eyes as I pressed the claims of Christ. Although she didn't make any decision right then, it wasn't long until Gloria gave her heart and life to the Saviour.

And then things were different. She was a new person: old things had passed away and all things had become new.

A few months later I saw Gloria again and I asked her about her "Hollywood career."

"Oh, Dr. Narramore," she said, "stop kidding me. I

haven't the least desire in the world to be in show business. I want to serve the Lord."

And she did. After high school and Bible College, she went to a foreign country (with a handsome husband) to serve as a staff musician on a Christian radio station. Now Gloria is in a job where her talents actually lie. She has achieved *real* success. Think what would have happened if God had not changed her desire for a theatrical profession. Hollywood and Hell, divorce, heartbreak, sin, mental anguish—another precious soul on the ash heap of sin and sorrow.

Direction? Yes! God points the way to success. But even *more* than that. He walks the road *with* you. For when God comes into a man's life, He actually goes into *partnership* with him. Human beings were never intended to go through life alone. They need the fellowship of God, their Creator. And when they are in fellowship with Him, they can face life victoriously knowing that they are on the winning side with God and therefore cannot fail.

Bill is a good example of what happens when we are in partnership with God. Bill had struggled along, making little if any headway. Then one day he met a fellow who encouraged him to come to church.

Why not? Bill thought. *I've tried everything else.*

He came and was intensely interested; then he came again.

Not long afterward the church conducted special evangelistic services. Bill came but he was *most* uncomfortable—until midway in the meetings when he made a decision for Christ and was wonderfully saved. After the meetings ended, Bill began to study the Bible with his new-found Christian friends. He grew in the Lord and became a changed fellow. Everything seemed different now. And it was.

His job? Well, actually he was doing the same work as he had before but his attitude was different. Now

Bill was working for and with Jesus, his Lord and Saviour.

A few years later Bill was transferred to the great Northwest. Here he continued to work for the same commercial company to pay expenses, but he was also working for God. He bought a bus and on Sundays he filled it with children from rural areas and brought them to church and Sunday school. He started an active home missionary project, working evenings, Sundays and during vacations. Yes, Bill was doing a big job for God.

Now Bill is one of the most successful men in the world. And it all began when he went into partnership with God.

The Right Kind of Success

Real success can only be measured by the dimensions of eternity, not by our tiny little piece of life here on earth. This is true because human beings have eternal souls that will live somewhere forever. The vital question is not "if." It is "where"—in Heaven or in Hell?

Things take on a different perspective and sense of values when we view them in terms of eternity. Our human view is so limited and so faulty. But God's view has an eternal dimension and it is as accurate as truth itself. This contrast between man's view and God's might be expressed something like this:

On earth we cannot always tell who is successful and who is not. But the facts come to light in eternity. A dramatic example is given in the Bible. God tells us that there was a certain rich man. (His name was not recorded. Evidently he wasn't successful enough to make God's "Who's Who.") This man had everything, a beautiful home, servants, fine clothes—and he lived off the fat of the land. By all the standards of the world, he was successful.

In contrast to this rich man was Lazarus—a poor, dependent beggar. He didn't have any of this world's goods. We do not know what unfortunate circumstances may have caused him to be in this pitiful state. But this we know, not only was he poverty-stricken but he was broken in health; and we are told that "the dogs came and licked his sores." A failure? In the eyes of his fellow men he was no doubt worse than that.

But in God's sight things were completely different. It took eternity to shed the proper light and perspective on the successes and failures of these two men. The rich man died and was buried. I can well imagine the elaborate burial ceremony for this man and the flowery inscriptions placed upon his tombstone. No doubt he was entombed with costly spices in a magnificent marble vault. But with all of this show of wealth, his soul was in hell suffering torment that exceeded all imagination.

On the other hand, when Lazarus died he was carried by the angels into Abraham's bosom. It is doubtful that this beggar even had a decent burial. But that didn't matter—that formality was only for the earthly body that was left behind. Now it was the *soul* that counted. And evidently his soul was in fellowship with God.

Was the rich man successful? Not in the light of eternity. His success was as short as his life. He had made no preparation for the soul that would live on forever.

No, Lazarus may not have succeeded in the eyes of men, but his success was measured by a heavenly goal. And throughout eternity he reaped the benefits of his wise choice. Did the wealthy man find no home in heaven because he was rich? Did the poor man find favor with God because he was poor? No, their bank accounts were not relevant, except for the impressions they made while here on earth.

So it is that in God's sight a seemingly insignificant person may be highly successful. In what way? Just think of that frail, obscure little old lady, who continually makes her petitions known before the Throne of Grace. A successful, joyous ministry? Indeed! Treasures? Yes, she has them—not in this earth, but in heaven where she can enjoy them for all eternity!

It Can Be You

Most of us have average ability, but it is surprising what great successes God can make out of very ordinary people. In His sight it is not the amount of talent that a person has that counts: rather, it is his yieldedness. And when God is moulding a life, you can be sure it will be successful.

I recall two high school boys who gave their hearts to Christ. As the months went by they both began to grow spiritually. Don was a tall, handsome boy who distinguished himself as an all-state athlete, and as an accomplished musician. He also had unusual abilities as a speaker. Everyone who knew him recognized his superior talents. In contrast, David was a homely boy from an extremely poor family. He had no special gifts or abilities. One might almost say that he was characterized by his mediocrity.

But the years following graduation brought many opportunities for life decisions. Christian friends began to see that Don was not including Christ in his plans while David sought the Lord in all that he did.

Some years later these young men presented an impressive comparison. It was evident that Don had not grown spiritually since his high school days. He was most unhappy, having had serious difficulties in several marriages, and not attaining success in either athletics or music. He had aged far beyond his years and was disillusioned and discouraged.

On the other hand, there was David, of only average ability—but what a contrast! He had not only received further Christian training, but he was happily married and busily engaged in a pastorate where he was being used mightily of God. David was thrilled with life, while Don could hardly bear it! David's happiness came not from natural attributes or from worldly acclaim but from being in the will of God.

Every sincere child of God can be and should be a success. For when God is in charge, there can be no failure. The apostle Paul said, "I can do *all* things through Christ who strengtheneth me" (Phil. 4:13). And we can say the same today.

What a wonderful thought—to know that we as believers have this special, supernatural help to make us successful. When we live close to the Lord, read His Word, pray and follow Him, we have the only recipe for genuine success. It is the promise of God: "This book of the law shall not depart out of thy mouth, but thou shalt meditate therein day and night that thou mayest observe to do according to all that is written therein; for then thou shalt make thy way prosperous, and then thou shalt have good success" (Josh. 1:8).

Success That Lasts Forever

"Laugh and the world laughs with you—cry and you cry alone."

How true! When we're on *top,* the world is with us: but let the picture change and we stand *alone.*

There is nothing much more vacillating than worldly success. Human nature is *fickle*—and since man measures success by the opinion of others, it becomes an insecure thing that can be lost in a minute's time.

Not long ago I heard a man give this definition of success: "Getting along with those you have to and keeping ahead of the rest of them." If this were true, a successful man is in the same precarious position as "humpty-dumpty." As long as he can sit on the wall, he is all right. But if he should fall off, his success is shattered.

I think of a friend of mine who was a great athlete. He was a famous miler—a runner who had set a new world's record and then, with lightning speed, had repeatedly broken his own record. He had won recognition and popular acclaim. Everywhere he went, people eyed him with admiration and asked for his autograph. He was crowned with success; he was riding the crest of popularity.

One day someone asked him, "How does it feel to be so successful?"

The athlete smiled wryly as he answered, "To be sure, there's a great thrill in being successful. And there's satisfaction in winning.

"But," he continued, "success doesn't last long. Sure—the crowd is with you, wildly applauding, screaming, stamping and yelling with enthusiasm; that is, as long as you're the winner. But when the day comes that you fail to knock off another fraction of a second from your time, or find that another runner can challenge your supremacy—then it's a different story. The crowd changes loyalties and, in no time at all, you are the forgotten man."

The forgotten man? Can this be true when only yesterday found him the world's hero?

Yes, it is true. One night we may shine with dazzling brilliance: but soon the spotlight is on someone else and we are not seen at all.

But there is success that doesn't fade! And God tells us about it in the Bible, His inspired Word. For in the book of Daniel, chapter 12, verse 3, we read: "And they that be wise shall shine as the brightness of the firmament; and they that turn many to righteousness as the stars forever and ever."

Here God shows us another dimension of success.

That dimension is "time." He says that the wise (those who win souls) and those who serve God by turning the unsaved to Him, shall SHINE! Not for a day, a year, or a season, not for a few years here on earth. But they shall shine through all *eternity*. Not only shall they shine as the stars forever and ever, but the quality of their brightness shall be as the firmament itself!

Have you ever watched a display of fireworks—perhaps on a Fourth of July night? Of course. The night is clear and starlit. Everyone is waiting. Then the fireworks begin! Some pop while others crackle, boom or shriek. But the noise is outdone only by the spectacular flashes of light. The rockets zoom upward, then burst into a blaze of multi-colored lights. Fountains of shimmering light fill the heavens. Beautiful streaks of fire blaze their paths across the midnight sky. Each one vies for prominence while the amazed crowd applauds with wild enthusiasm.

But an hour or so later the noise stops. The fireworks are gone. The rockets are silent and there is not a trace of the temporary display. And now, as you look into the sky again, you see the stars! There they are as bright and brilliant as before. And—permanent. Their glory was momentarily forgotten with the noise and success of the temporary flashes of man. But centuries later the *stars will still be shining*.

So it is with temporary, earthly success. At best it is only a feeble rocket which creates a momentary stir in the minds of men. Then it is forgotten. But, God promises that those who are godly and "wise" and those "that turn many to righteousness" shall be as the "stars forever and ever."

Sometimes we see godly men and women who seem to be insignificantly hidden by the razzle-dazzle of men. Perhaps a shop worker, a daily laborer, a school boy, an obscure preacher or a missionary, or a humble prayer warrior on a bed of suffering. And when we see these "little people of God" and compare them with the "big shots" of television, the prominent names of science, the luminaries of Hollywood or the "wheels" of politics, we wonder why God's own are not "successful."

THEY ARE SUCCESSFUL, but *we* are the ones who do not have the *eternal perspective*. For remember, God who speaks with eternity in view says that these lowly, godly saints shall *SHINE AS THE BRIGHTNESS OF THE FIRMAMENT, AS THE STARS THAT SHINE FOREVER AND EVER!*

10
Faith That Endures

"THERE I WAS, dangling in space. Millions of miles from nowhere.

"Oh, what a terrible, hopeless feeling! Nothing to hold on to, nothing to reach or grab. I didn't have the least idea where I was. There was no up, no down, no sides, no corners—just endless nothingness."

This is how one client described his dream—a veritable "nightmare" that troubled him night after night. But as we talked it through, he found that these dreams were the exaggerated "left-overs" of his daily feelings—distortions of his unresolved conflicts.

There is nothing worse than groping—"hopelessly dangling." Everyone needs to feel that he has something to which he can anchor. Continual uncertainty is mental torture.

Our space age society bears several trademarks. One of them is insecurity. People want to be secure. Financially secure, secure in their family relationships, secure in their jobs and secure in their social standing. But the most important security is often overlooked. Only in recent years have psychologists and psychiatrists begun to analyze man with a new dimension in mind. This new important dimension is "Faith." "Faith in a Supreme Being," they say, "brings stability and security." Indeed, an enduring faith in the living God is basic to all other "securities" in life. On this hinges the whole pattern of our life—now and for eternity.

As a psychologist, I realize that this is one of our basic needs. But it is not enough to have faith. We must have a *secure* faith—one that is certain today, tomorrow and throughout eternity.

It is a psychological fact that people are healthier and happier when they are *secure*. How would you feel if you were not sure that you owned your car? How would you feel if you didn't know whether you were married? How would you feel if you were indefinite about your employment—not sure of a pay check? To function normally and to function well, a human being must know where he stands. Extreme insecurity results in a disorganized mind which may lead to mental illness.

Yet there are many people (even sincere Christians) who are not *secure*. Their spiritual life is shaky, as though they were walking on the brink of a frightful precipice. Faith in God? Yes, but not a *secure* faith. They *hope* they are going to heaven. They *trust* that someday they will "make the Pearly Gates"; they *think* they may "cross over Jordan"; they *presume* they will some day see God.

But deep down inside they are not sure! In reality they are waiting until they die to see what actually will happen to them. And their fate is a mystery that is sealed until death.

No one knows better than God, our Creator, how harmful it is for man to continually feel uncertain. God never intended for His creatures to be insecure; and man never was—until he sinned and turned his back on God, the very source of all certainty and security.

God didn't let it go at that, however. In His great love, He made a marvelous provision for mankind, so that they need not grope blindly for something on which they might stake their future. Nor does God want them to. God made the supreme sacrifice—He gave His own Son, Jesus Christ, to die for our sins. When we trust in His shed blood we are forgiven. We are then the sons of God—and we are assured of an eternity with Him.

There is no guesswork about this. It is sure. As sure as God Himself.

If, of course, you are trusting in your own "good" works, or religious observances, or pious feelings, or your own moral standards—you are trying to get in by a back door and it will not work. Jesus spoke very plainly about this. He said, "I am the door: by me if any man enters in, he shall be saved, and shall go in and out, and find pasture" (John 10:9). He also said, "He that entereth not by the door into the sheepfold but climbeth up some other way, the same is a thief and a robber" (John 10:1).

A thief and a robber! If ever there is a picture of *insecurity*, this is it. When people look to themselves, or their relatives or to an organization or to some "great" leader for their salvation, they are by-passing the crucified Christ, the only means of security. And they will never know genuine security that leads to happiness.

There is only *one* provision for salvation. It is through a personal relationship with Jesus. God says, "There is none other name under heaven given among men, whereby we must be saved" (Acts 4:12). "Believe on the Lord Jesus Christ, and thou shalt be saved" (Acts 16:31). Believe! Not *do*. "For by grace are ye saved, through faith; and that not of yourselves: it is the gift of God: Not of works, lest any man should boast" (Eph. 2:8, 9).

Since salvation is the *gift of God*, could anything be more secure? All we need to do is to *accept* this gift and our souls are secure. With Him, there is no such thing as "dangling." Insecurity is completely opposed to God's nature. He is the author of all security. *He is complete security*. Nothing, absolutely nothing in this world can compare with the security we have in God.

I was born and raised on a western ranch. As a boy I was fascinated by the beautiful majestic mountains that surrounded our fertile valley. They were always there, and always the same. True, they changed their hues to blend with the moods of the day—blue in the morning, gray at noonday, pink and purple in the evening. But they never changed their form or their location. They were sure, they were solid—they seemed almost eternal. Other things changed. The trees and the shrubs grew or were cut down. New homes dotted the landscape, old ones were removed. New highways cut through the fields. The people grew older. Some moved away and others took their place. But through the years the mountains remained—unchanged.

Today when I visit the little community of my boyhood, I am still impressed with the mountains. The years have changed nearly everything else, but the mountains seem the same. Little wonder that writers and poets call them the "eternal" mountains. It is understandable why a great insurance company uses a famous mountain, the Rock of Gibraltar, as its symbol of dependability and security.

But rocks and mountains are *not* indestructible, Steadfast and unmovable as they seem to be, they surrender to nature and to man. Earthquakes can shake them, volcanoes can erupt them, wind and water can erode them, and man can blast them or mine them away.

There is nothing sure and certain except God. He is from everlasting to everlasting. His Word endureth forever. When our faith is placed in His hands, it is *secure* beyond our finite understanding.

I remember Phil's experience. Phil was one of my professional associates. Once a week several of the men from the office had lunch together in a nearby park. There, around a picnic table, we "munched" and had a little Bible study. One day while we were talking and eating lunch, Phil confided, "Well men, I hate to make this confession, but I don't know whether I'm really saved or not."

The men looked up, and one of them asked, "What do you mean?"

"Just what I said," replied Phil. "I've gone to church all my life. In fact, I've taught classes and I've even been the superintendent of the Sunday school. But I can't say for *sure* that I'm saved. And what really disturbs me is the fact that you men all talk as if you know definitely that you are saved. I might as well confess right here and now that I don't have that assurance."

"Let's take a look at what God has to say about it," I suggested.

So we opened the Book and looked at I John 5:12. "He that hath the Son hath life; and he that hath not the Son of God hath not life."

"Well," said Phil, "I never knew that was in the Bible."

Then we looked at the next verse, I John 5:13. "These things have I written unto you that believe on the name of the Son of God; that ye may *know* that ye have eternal life, and that ye may *believe* on the name of the Son of God."

We read the verse several times. "Phil," I said, "do you see at least two very important things in this verse? One is the fact that God has given us the written Word so that we might *believe* on His name. Another important fact is that He has given us this written Word so that after we believe on His name, we might *know* for sure that we have eternal life.

"*BELIEVE* and *KNOW*. Isn't that marvelous? God doesn't want us to be uncertain or perplexed. He says in His own Word that we can be saved and *know* it."

"That's right," agreed the other men.

Phil looked up. "Do you think there are many people who are saved and who don't know it for certain?" he asked.

"Yes," I nodded, "I'm sure there are. You see, it's one thing to be saved, but it's still another thing to have the assurance through His Word—to know beyond the shadow of a doubt that you have eternal life. Let's take one more look at God's Word."

We turned the pages to John 10:28 where we read:

"And I give unto them eternal life; and they shall never perish, neither shall any man pluck them out of my hand."

"That says the same thing three times," commented Phil. "God says that He gives unto us eternal life—life that never ends, then He says that we shall never perish, and then He says that no one will ever be able to pluck us out of His hand."

"That's right," the men agreed.

"Well," said Phil, "since I actually don't know whether I am saved or not I'd like to make sure right now."

Then Phil quietly bowed his head and prayed this simple prayer, "Lord, come into my heart and save me. If I have never before given my life to You, I am doing so right now. Please forgive me of my sins—and be my Lord. And thank You for doing it. In Jesus' name I pray. Amen."

That was a precious time for all of us.

From that moment on Phil was sure, not because of his feelings, but because God's eternal Word said so. Interestingly enough that day marked a great change in his life. Spiritually he began to grow and develop.

A few months later when I was talking with Phil I asked him whether he still had his "know-so" salvation.

"Of course I do," he said. "Ever since that day in the park when I settled it all, there's never been a doubt in my mind."

"But how can you be sure?" I questioned.

"Because God says so in His Word."

Absolutely! Phil was right. There is nothing more certain than God's Word—"Heaven and earth shall pass away, but my words shall not pass away" (Matt. 24:35).

But Phil's case was not at all unusual. Many people have this problem.

It was a real problem with Jon. A few years ago I flew up to Iceland on a speaking tour. The first day I was introduced to Jon, a tall, blonde fellow, typically Nordic, chauvinistic, and in every sense an Icelander. Jon was to be my pianist for our two weeks' stay. The first afternoon we got together and talked over our music plans. During the conversation I asked, "Jon, do you know for sure that you are saved?"

"Oh," he answered, "I know it as well as anyone could possibly know it *without dying*."

"What do you mean?"

"Well, being saved is something that you cannot be positive about until you die."

"Oh, is that right? Listen very carefully tonight, Jon."

That night I brought a message on the assurance of salvation. And at the end of the service Jon came to me and shook my hand. "I want to thank you," he said, "for coming to Iceland. This is only the first night, but already your trip has been a success!"

"What do you mean, Jon?"

"Well, up until tonight I was not *certain* whether I was saved. But while you were speaking, God spoke to my heart and I realized then that I *could* know for sure. So I asked Him to come into my life and to save me. I knew that if I had never been born again before, I wanted to be, so I settled it right then and there. Now I am sure," he said, "and I am the happiest person in the world. This is what I've been looking for—and now I've found it."

"What's your basis for knowing?" I asked.

"The Bible," he answered.

And Jon was exactly right.

Yes, you too can trust in Christ and know for certain that you are saved.

"But," you may wonder, "*how* can I know?"

How? Simply by reading God's Word and believing it. If God says so, that is enough. You can depend upon His Word. It is settled in heaven—*forever!* See Ps. 119:89.

"Hath He said, and shall He not do it? or hath He spoken, and shall He not make it good?" (Num. 23:19).

It is not a matter of the quantity or quality of your faith. The question is how trustworthy is the person in whom you place your confidence. Is his character beyond reproof? Is he absolutely truthful? Is he 100% dependable? As much as we like our friends, we must admit that they are imperfect. By nature people are sinful and because of this even with all their fine attributes they are not always dependable.

But the character of God is beyond reproach. He is perfect: He is just: He is Holy. And God's Word is as sure as His character. "If we receive the witness of men, the witness of God is greater: for this is the witness of God which he hath testified of his Son . . . He that believeth not God hath made him a liar; because he believeth not the record that God gave of his Son" (I John 5:9, 10). "Abraham believed God, and it was counted unto him for righteousness" (Rom. 4:3).

A distressed lady once came to her minister. She was uncertain as to whether she was actually saved. "Oh pastor," she sighed, "I can't believe!"

"Can't believe whom?" the pastor asked.

She looked up, startled! She had never thought of it that way before. By refusing to believe, she was doubting God.

Faith is not something that we must feel within us. It is the committing of ourselves to someone else—to God. We may say that we have faith in a ship to carry us across the ocean. But it is not until we board the ship that we actually exercise our faith. Once we commit ourselves to the ship, it makes little difference how much we believe in its ability to sail safely to the other shore. It will carry the doubter just as securely as it does the one who completely trusts. But the worried doubter will miss out on the joy of the journey.

So it is with the Christian. When he trusts in Christ as his Saviour, he is saved even though he may feel uncertain about it. But unfortunately he misses out on the blessing. This is not God's will. Because in His Word He clearly tells us over and over again that we can *know* that we are saved.

Sometimes people ask, "Doesn't a person receive the assurance of his salvation at the time he is saved?" And of course the answer is: he may; but he may not. It depends largely upon whether the new convert reads this great truth in God's Word and whether the person leading him to Christ points it out to him.

Undoubtedly some people are saved who do not have the assurance of salvation. On the other hand there are people who do not have the assurance of salvation because they actually are not saved yet. But this is a fact: *Anyone who is saved can know it. And anyone who is in doubt can certainly make sure!*

I remember when I received the assurance of *my* salvation. I had trusted in Christ as my personal Saviour. And immediately afterward I began to read God's Word daily. It wasn't long until the Holy Spirit through the Scriptures began to witness to me about my salvation. God seemed to use one particular portion of Scripture to seal this truth to my heart. It was John 5:24. "Verily, verily, I say unto you, He that heareth my Word, and believeth on Him that sent me, hath everlasting life, and shall not come into condemnation; but is passed from death unto life."

"Heareth my Word, and *believeth* on Him that sent

me." Yes, I thought. *I've done that. I've truly heard His Word, the Bible, and I have believed.*

Then God spoke to me about the next word: "hath." I knew that "hath" meant "has." Has everlasting life! Tomorrow? Someday? When I die? No, *has right now!*

Then God led me to the next phrase: "And shall not come into condemnation." *No condemnation in the future,* I thought. *How wonderful! I shall not come into condemnation and judgment.*

Then God led me further to the last phrase: "But is passed from death unto life." *Is passed.* Gone. Already settled. Passed from what? From death unto life. "I have God's new life!"

Then I read the verse over and over. The truths flooded my mind: The one who hears and believes *HAS* eternal life—*now.* And he shall not come into condemnation but he *IS PASSED* already from death unto life!

Then I bowed my head and heart in prayerful thanksgiving. "I never need to worry," I said to myself. "It is settled forever. Now my responsibility is to serve Him the best I can as long as I live." Yes, that is how God spoke to me.

The story is told of two men who were journeying on their camels across the vast sandy regions of the Sahara desert. Slowly they made their way across the thirsty wilderness, following the footprints of an earlier caravan. Suddenly a violent sandstorm swept across the barren land and the two travelers were forced to take shelter in a nearby cave. The fierce, hot winds blew the sand and gravel until the men were scarcely able to see the camels by their side. At length the storm subsided, and all was serene once more. But as the men looked out across the wilderness the picture had changed completely. Every sand dune had shifted. Every shrub was covered. The few, meager landmarks were gone. One of the travelers, seeking in vain for some tracks, finally threw up his hands in utter dismay and exclaimed, "We are lost, we are hopelessly lost."

The other traveler had nothing to say. But that night after the sun sank beyond the western horizon, he gazed up into the star studded velvet of the night and said, "No, we are *not* lost. The stars are still there!"

So it is with us. The rapidly changing landscape of this stormy world may dismay us. The people we trust may fail us. And we may despair, feeling that we are hopelessly lost. But when we look up toward God rather than at our earthly surroundings, we can see that *the stars are still there*. Surely, if God can throw millions of stars into the sky, can hold all things together, and keep the universe moving with minute precision, we can rest assured that He is not haphazard about our eternal destiny. God's Word is more dependable than anything else in the universe. And when He is the guardian of our souls, we can be at peace knowing that we are indeed secure—without the shadow of a doubt.

This is *faith that endures.* This is God's way—to happiness!